“Jash”

Name In The Sky!

Jash E. Lardie

ISBN: 979-8-89663-052-4

Dedication

I dedicate this book, my life's story, to all the good people of this world who truly care about truth and justice!

May this world not corrupt you, but may you finish your life's race with dignity and honor!

Acknowledgment

I thank God Almighty, the Creator of all the universe, for always being there for me, even when the entire world seemed to turn its back on me. Thank you, Jesus, for your friendship, forgiveness, mercy, love, and grace! And for being the biggest and best part of my life!

About the Author

Jash has been a praise and worship leader, sung in three different church choirs, and plays the keyboard, guitar, and drums. He has served as a youth pastor, assistant pastor, and lead pastor, and is also a street evangelist. His greatest joy is serving the Kingdom of Heaven and Jesus Christ. His only weakness might be his incredibly compassionate heart; he'll go to great lengths to help anyone.

Preface

This is the second and special edition of my autobiography. The purpose of this "Special Edition" is to engage the reader in participating, to help get the government to do the right thing; which is to exonerate and compensate me for the incredible wrongs it did to me.

The original intent of telling my story is to make known what actually happened. The corrupt judicial system and fake news media lied to the public in huge ways. My goal is to bring awareness to these injustices and to prevent any further injustices from occurring. I am not the only victim of these out-of-control entities. Lastly, and most importantly, my story informs people how to obtain eternal life. One must only do what I did to guarantee yourself a place in heaven.

Contents

Introduction

The most horrifying event in my entire life left a hole in my soul, bigger than I ever thought possible. One moment life can be all peaches and cream, and out of nowhere, life can turn absolutely dark in no time at all. I am a very optimistic person, and I hate to dwell on the negative things in life, but one can never completely drown out the darkness. It is not mentally healthy, to focus on the negative things that happen to us or to dwell too much on what bad can happen. It is also not healthy to pretend everything is all peaches and cream all of the time either. There is a healthy balance. I do have to say though, the dark hole in my soul has found a marvelous light and perfect peace to fill it. Whatever hole, and/or darkness that may have made its way into your life, I truly believe my story will help you find healing and peace as well.

Chapter 1
"My Early Years"

My name is Jash. No, that is not a type-o. Many people mistake my name as Josh, but like I have told thousands of people, "It is Jash; Josh with an 'A'". It rhymes with ash, bash, cash, dash, flash, gash, lash, mash, rash, stash, trash, etc.....

I was born into a very loving family in a small American city called Traverse City, in the beautiful state of Michigan - the state that looks like a hand. My parents loved children, I can't emphasise that enough. My earliest childhood memories are of my mother's home daycare. Between the daycare and the numerous kids in our neighborhood, our house always had lots of kids in it.

Our house was the house most of the neighborhood children liked to hang out at. I believe this was mainly to do with how loving and kind my parents were and partly because my father built us the coolest tree house ever. This tree house was the envy of not just our neighborhood, but also of other surrounding neighborhoods. It had three windows that opened, a door that locked and a carpeted floor. It was suspended around 12 feet in the air, but if you climbed on top of its roof, you were closer to 20 feet up toward the sky. In the summer months, my brother and I often had friends stay the night, and we would sleep in the tree fort. As for siblings, I only had one; it was just my one younger brother and myself. I grew up surrounded by friends, a small loving family, and pets. We had lots and lots of pets growing up. We never had much money at all. Both of my parents worked full time jobs all their lives, but still never had much money. We spent most of our extra money going on vacations around the United States which almost always consisted of driving and camping. We rarely flew or stayed in hotels. We did a lot of things together as a family. We would go on family trips, play cards and board games on a regular basis, and went camping quite often. One of my childhood joys was going fishing with my dad. My dad loved to fish. He taught me to fish at a very early age. I would say that I came from a very healthy family. My parents had two of the biggest hearts I have ever seen in people. My parents were 19 and 21 years old when they had me.

Being the oldest sibling, I grew up fairly quickly. I was momma's big helper with the daycare children and was often the babysitter of my younger brother. I learned to take care of pets at an early age and had my first job at the age of eleven delivering newspapers 6 days a week. The paper route made me strong and fast. I would strap two newspaper bags over my shoulders and run my route as fast as I could. In sixth grade, my school let me go home early and skip our day's last recess so that I could deliver my newspapers before track started. I would run home, deliver my papers as fast as I could, then run back to school to run track. The paper route was my warm-up for track.

By ninth grade, I was the second fastest kid out of seven hundred kids in my school's grade level. I joined track in eleventh grade only to quickly drop out of it. By this time, I was sixteen years old and working for a restaurant. My track coach said I was a fast runner and told me that I could run my way through college on a scholarship, but to do so, I needed to quit my job and also quit smoking. He said the only reason I needed a job was to pay for my car, and that the only reason I needed a car was to get to work; that it was an endless cycle, and that I should instead run for a scholarship.

He then told me, since I had a painful case of shin splints, that I should only run two miles that day. I saw the two miles as torture being that my legs hurt so bad that they felt like they were going to fall right off of me, and to quit my job and give up my car seemed like such a big sacrifice at that point in my life. The coach did not understand; my car got me to my friends' houses and to parties, not just to work each day. To be in the social circle, I was in; I needed my car. To get rid of my car would be social suicide for me. Besides that, I saved up my money for a number of years on my paper route to buy my car. Not to mention, my mother took a second job and worked nights to help me buy a nice car. She matched me a dollar per dollar to buy a nicer car than I could have afforded by myself. I was introduced to alcohol, cigarettes, marijuana, and LSD at age fifteen. The good chunk of money I had saved from delivering papers for four years made me many new friends. These friends were helping me spend my money on alcohol and drugs. My family moved out of our childhood house and neighborhood when I was fifteen and into a rental house while we were building a new house ourselves. These new friends of mine from my new neighborhood really took me in a different direction in life. The drinking and drugs made bowling on a league no longer fun to me, and when the track coach asked me to give up smoking and partying, he was asking a whole lot from me. Besides, I didn't think I could quit smoking even if I wanted to. Instead of quiting my job, I decided to quit track instead. This was one of the many mistakes I made in life.

I also bowled on a league every year from age 5 to age 16. We won first place the first team I was on and the last team I was on, as well as many times in between those two teams. My bowling average was at an all-time high of 218 around the time that I quit bowling which was good enough to go pro.

At age fifteen, even though I had a much better paying job working at a restaurant, versus having a paper route, my mother saw that my bank account was quickly going in the wrong direction. She said that I needed to buy a car soon before my money was all gone. We purchased a car for me even before I was legally old enough to drive. I remember having the car in our driveway, even though I was not allowed by law to drive it yet. I would dream of the day that I could drive legally. While we were out of town building our new house, my parents would let me drive their car down to the outhouses even though I was not old enough to drive legally. There were never really any cops around to bust me for driving out where we were building our house. By the time I was old enough to take a driver's education class, I was already a pretty good driver; so much so, that the instructor I had said that I did not even need to practice in the school's parking lot before I hit the road for a road test. I think he just saw how confident I was riding along with other students in my class and how I flinched and sighed each time they did something wrong.

My parents taught me to be a very loving and compassionate person. They told me I should never lend money out but instead, give it to people. If the people want to pay you back, that is on them. My mother told me that lending money to people often causes friendships to fall apart. They also taught me never to hit anyone. I got good at restraining people, versus hitting them, and I gave to many people who were in need, without expecting anything in return.

Chapter 2
"First Run-in's with the Law"

Within the first two years of getting my driver's license, I had five run-ins with the law. Two of the run-ins with the law were simple speeding tickets. A third driving ticket was for driving too fast for road conditions. I slid just enough around an icy corner and dented an El Camino that a guy had just restored. An El Camino looks like a cross between a car and a small pick-up truck. The guy took me to court to sue me for damages, but my mom worked at an insurance company and knew he could only get a few hundred dollars even though he wanted much more.

My mom approached the judge and gave him paperwork that showed that our state was a no-fault insurance state and that the guy could only get a little amount of money. The judge got sassy with my mother and told her that he knew this. She asked why then were they even allowing this guy to take me to court being the guy was going to have to pay his attorney more than he could even get from the accident? It was my first experience seeing how wrong the courts were.

My fourth run-in with the law was for smoking marijuana while driving to school. Two undercover police officers, or off-duty police officers, saw us smoking the now legal drug while on our way to school. The cops took one of my passengers into their car. This passenger's dad was an undercover drug officer. He got in no trouble at all. The police had me drive my car down to the police station while they followed us. We were arrested, booked and then immediately released. I received a ticket for possession of marijuana and was given a court date. I did not understand how I was given a ticket for possession when I had no drugs in my possession. The police told me that when they saw me smoking the drug I was in possession at that time. To make a long story short, they reduced the ticket/charge to use of marijuana when I went to probate (children's) court. I was given probation and made to do some community service hours.

My fifth run-in with the law was a bit more interesting to me, and a bit more eye-opening. A friend of mine and I went out one night and trespassed. Well, we did quite a bit more than that, but I do not wish to incriminate myself even though I am sure that the statute of limitations is well over by now. The one thing that I will confess to, is that we crawled under a fence and looked around a factory's work yard. I was very curious, of what they had under the big dark government looking tarps. I pulled up one tarp to get a look at what was under it. All I saw was some foreign looking metal object. I believed it was a part of a NASA space shuttle. While looking at the unidentified metal object, my friend came over and grabbed me by the arm and said we had to run, that there was a magnetic alarm. I was not sure what he meant at the time, because I did not know what a magnetic alarm was, but I took off running with him because of how fearful he appeared. We shortly thereafter, saw a cop car drive past by the alley we were walking down. We took off when the cop put his car in reverse and shined a spotlight at us. We ran across a few yards and into my friend's house. We then quickly ran upstairs and jumped into his bed. About 10 minutes later, the police broke into his house, came upstairs and arrested us. We were immediately separated and hauled off to jail. I heard my friend yelling at the cops about how they can't just burst into his dad's house and arrest us. They said they were in hot pursuit and thus allowed to enter the premises without his dad's permission.

Once we were inside separate police cars, they told both of us that the other one had already confessed to everything; and that we might as well just come clean about everything we had done. I began to get really scared because of the amount of crimes we had committed that night. I had no reason to not believe that the police were telling the truth and thought that we were in a lot of trouble. They said that they knew we had broken into the factory's building because they had seen our wet footprints inside the building. As far as I knew, my friend had never gone into the building. If he had gone in, it was only for a second, for he had only left my side for literally a few seconds, so I was sure he hadn't walked around much inside of it. The police then said that they had seen us when we were hiding behind a parked truck, and that we were lucky they didn't see something shinny in our hands or they might have shot us. I knew they were lying about seeing us behind the truck, or else they would have seen what my friend stole from the truck, and they would have arrested us at that very moment. There was a fresh snowfall out that night; the police had followed our footprints in the snow. That was how they knew my friend had stepped a few feet into the building, it is also how they knew we had stood behind a parked truck, and it is also how they found out what house we were in. I figured out that the only thing they really knew about was the trespassing at the factory, so I confessed to that crime.

I still had a fear that my friend may have confessed to more than just the trespassing crime, so when we were allowed to see each other at the police station/jail, we both asked each other what we had really said to police. He also had confessed to the trespassing and told them he just opened the door to the building. We were both very relieved to know that neither of us had told the police anything else we had done wrong that night like the police said we had. I didn't know police would use lying as a tactic. It is illegal to lie to the police, but apparently, it is not illegal for them to lie to us. It was an eye-opener to me, to see that the police will lie to people to get them to confess to crimes they otherwise don't know about. What was even more of an eye-opener, was what took place once we had to go to court for the crime.

When I had to go to court for the trespassing crime I committed, I was more than ready to face the consequences for my wrongdoing. When the judge asked me how I wanted to plea at my arraignment, I told him that I would like to plead guilty. He suddenly looked shocked and dropped the papers he was holding in a very overdramatic manner. Then he told me, that I must not understand how the system works. He shouted out to the courtroom and asked if there was an attorney in the room who could give me some free legal advice. A real smug attorney said he would do it. The judge then told the attorney, to tell me what it was like to represent myself in the court of law without an attorney present. The attorney told me that representing myself in a court of law, was like doing brain surgery on myself with a mirror, and then asked me if I would do brain surgery on myself with a mirror? I told him that I would not. I didn't see a small misdemeanor charge for trespassing anywhere nearly as severe as brain surgery. It seemed to me that they were going a bit far with how big of a deal this all was.

The judge then said that I needed to plead not guilty and that he would then appoint me a court-appointed attorney. Then he said, "Mr. Lardie, I repeat myself, how would you like to plead today to the crime you have been charged with?" What? I could not understand this. I was raised to be an honest person. I was told not to lie to people, especially to those in authority. It was bad enough to discover that the police, one of our society's authorities, lied to me, now a judge was telling me to lie to him. I saw the judge as our community's biggest authority, and he wanted me to tell him that I was not guilty of a crime I knew I was guilty of. But I obeyed the judge and reluctantly pleaded not guilty. It all felt so wrong to me. The judge then displayed an evil looking grin and said that that was a better response, and then appointed me an attorney.

A few weeks later, I met my court appointed attorney. My attorney told me that I needed to go before the judge and just plead guilty for the trespassing crime, that because I had already confessed to the police that I had committed the crime, I had no case. I told the attorney that I could not plead guilty, that I had already tried to do so, but the judge said I cannot do that. The attorney told me that now that I had a real court date and an attorney, that I could now tell the truth instead of lying, and put in a guilty plea. This all seemed so backwards to me. Why couldn't I just tell the truth the first time I was before the judge?

At my next court appearance, I stood before the same judge and was asked the same question I was asked the first time I stood before him. I again told him that I was guilty. He then sentenced me to three nights in jail, to a period of probation and said I had to pay for my court appointed attorney. He said I would serve my three nights in a few weeks over a weekend. I asked him why I couldn't do my three nights the weekend that was upon us. He said he had never had anyone want to move their jail sentence up before and said it was fine by him. I was planning on going to Florida on the original weekend he wanted me to spend in jail. I wanted to get the sentence over as soon as possible, and not have it get in the way of my trip. The worst part of it all was that I had to pay for an attorney that I did not feel I ever needed in the first place.

My three days stay in our county jail was a new experience for me. When you are only doing a short sentence like I was, you are not thrown into the general population. I was put in a cell with inmates who were on work release. These inmates basically worked their normal jobs in society all day long and then just stayed the night in jail each night. I remember my very first conversation with one of these inmates. It was a frightening experience for me that I am not sure I will ever forget. I walked into the cell with my jail-issued blanket, which I placed on the only empty bunk bed and then walked up to the cell's television. I changed the channel since it appeared that no one was watching it. An inmate who was on a bottom bunk immediately rolled over and yelled at me in a mean loud voice for changing the station. I quickly turned the station back and apologized. I informed him that I didn't think anyone was watching it, after all, to my defense, he was faced in the opposite direction from the television, so I assumed he was sleeping. He then told me that he was listening to it and to not change the channel again.

I pretty much just kept to myself for the rest of my short jail sentence. Come to find out, a three-day sentence is only one full day and a small part of two other days. You check into the jail on a Friday night, then get out very early on Sunday morning. You really only stay in jail for one full day; Saturday. Shortly after checking in on Friday you go to sleep, you sleep in for as long as you can on Saturday, and on Sunday they kick you out before the sun rises.

Because I had the two speeding tickets, and then got a third driving ticket for driving too fast for weather conditions, I had to have a hearing at the Secretary of State to discuss my punishment from them. The outcome of this meeting was that I received a restricted driver's license. The restriction consisted of me not being allowed to drive between the hours of 11pm at night, and 6am in the morning. Because of this restriction, I allowed whoever I was out partying with to drive my car when it was past 11pm. This got me into the habit of letting a lot of people drive my car.

A lot of children my age did not have cars of their own yet. I felt quite taken advantage of because I owned my own car. I basically became a free taxi service for many kids around my age. I gave kids rides to school, then rides home after school. Some kids I gave rides to work, mostly those who worked with me. Almost every Friday and Saturday night I gave kids rides to parties, some of which I was not even allowed to attend. One girl had me wrapped around her little finger. She would call me up at work, beg me to come get her and take her to a party and then tell me to come pick her up later. I believe she was the second girl I ever kissed if not the first, and she knew she could get me to do anything.

Chapter 3
Before the Crash (B.C.)

I had a hard time telling people no when it came to people asking me for rides. As I had mentioned, I was basically a free taxi to many teenagers. Some of the kids would throw me a little money for gas, but for the most part, I gave people rides for free. I always liked to help people out who were in need. As I also mentioned, once I had my driving restriction and was not allowed to drive past 11pm at night, I would let whoever I was out with drive my car after 11pm.

I graduated high school one semester earlier than most of the rest of my graduating class. I was seventeen years old when I graduated and went straight into the full-time workforce after doing so. I had a full-time job working at a bakery. The main problem with working at a bakery, while trying to party on the weekends, was the fact that bakers need to start very early in the morning so that people can have fresh bread for the day. I would often go to work after only sleeping a few hours the night before, if I slept at all. There were a few occasions that I did not sleep at all and would just go straight to work.

The night before the accident, I had only slept a couple of hours. I had gone to a party that Friday night expecting to only hang out for a little while and then go home to sleep because I was throwing a party of my own the following night on Saturday. While at this party on Friday night in a wooden area, the police showed up and busted it. Somehow a girl my age that I barely knew wound up in my car needing a ride miles and miles away in the opposite direction of my house. By the time I got home that night, I only had 2 hours left to sleep before having to get up for work.

I went to work and told my boss how tired I was. He suggested I find a place in the woods to take a nap after work. I thought this was sort of a strange suggestion, but wish I had at least given it a try. There are a million and one things I wished I had done differently the night before and even hours before the accident. But wishes like these are pointless. You can't change the past. After I got home from work, I went out to the woods to cut up some firewood for my party. I ran a chainsaw for an hour or so mostly cutting up an old dead pine tree. The chainsaw would not stay running, and I had to continually keep pulling the starter cord, to the point that it rubbed my knuckles raw and physically wore me out.

After cutting up some wood for the fire I was planning on having that night, I walked back out of the valley up to our house to put the chainsaw away and to get a cooler for beer. Then I made a number of trips back and forth between our house and the cooler to put beer and ice into it. After working and prepping for my party, I was beyond exhausted. I went back to our house to take a bath, but my parents were home by this time, and my mother told me that I could not take a bath because she had just cleaned up the entire bathroom for the housewarming party they were throwing that night. I then went to go to my room to take a nap, but again, I was told people would be arriving soon and that I needed to get dressed and ready for their party. My family had just finished building a house ourselves. I was in a construction trades class at our high school for the last year and a half until I graduated. My family spent roughly six months prepping some wooded land to build a house on it and then spent the next six months building the house. We did most of it ourselves but also had a few occasions where a number of people came out to help us. One day my dad invited a number of people from the factory he worked at to come out and help when we put the roof's rafters up. Lots of other friends and family members came out on different occasions to help us out here and there.

As a form of appreciation to all the people that helped us, and also to celebrate the finishing of our brand-new house, my parents were throwing a housewarming party. I decided to throw a little party of my own that same night. My party was to be down in the valley and around a hill, which put it out of sight of our house and out of sight of my parent's party. I invited a good number of teenagers, mostly ranging from 15 to 19 years old. I didn't expect very many people to show up to my party. I had thrown a party a couple of months prior to this one and had only around 5 or 6 people show up. For the first party, I had thrown, I had bought enough beer for about 30 to 40 people. Being only 5 or 6 people showed up, I had a lot of beer left over. For this next party, I just got enough beer for around 5 to 10 people. My parents on the other hand expected to have upwards to over 100 people attend their party. As many people have discovered, life doesn't always go as planned.

Chapter 4
"The Party"

A few minutes before my parent's party was to start, my parents and I gathered in our garage where they had set up tables and chairs for gathering and eating at. Out of nowhere, my mother began to cry. My dad and I expressed concern and asked what the matter was. She then began to cry hysterically and yelled out that something bad was going to happen that night. My dad and I assured my mother that she had no way of knowing that this was true and that we thought everything would be fine.

Some of the first guests to arrive were for my party. I told them we were partying in the backyard and that they could go back there and hang out. We started my party by playing a game called "Hacky Sack". It is a game where everyone stands in a circle and uses their bodies to pass, pause and do other tricks with a little bean bag type of a ball the size of a golf ball. The game mostly consisted of kicking and using one's knees to keep the hacky sack in the air. The only part of your body that was off limits was your hands.

More and more kids began to show up for my party. My parent's guests began to arrive as well. I was surprised how many people were showing up for my party. Go figure, for the party I threw a few months earlier, I had lots of alcohol and only a few guests came, and now that I only had a little alcohol, I had lots of guests showing up. There were actually a lot more guests showing up, then were even invited. My guests were bringing guests, and the guests they brought had invited other guests who also were showing up. Basically, my party got crashed. Lots and lots of people showed up to party!

I didn't care so much that lots of kids were coming who I had not personally invited, or even knew for that matter. I always believe in the saying, "The more, the merrier." A friend I had invited brought some fifths of alcohol, and some other guests brought some drugs, but for the most part, I did not have nearly enough alcohol to give each of them even one drink.

I began running back and forth between my parent's party and my own party. I would say hello to some of my relatives and friends of my parents, then run back down to the party that I was hosting. At one point I got the idea to steal some of my parents' alcohol. I ran some beer down to my party and threw it into my cooler, but faster than I could even fill my color, it would empty right back out. I could not keep running back and forth between the two parties because of how completely exhausted I was. At one point I told some of my guests that they could find lots of alcohol up in my parents' garage. I told them to go and grab some and bring it down to our party. I had backed my car down to my party and opened the trunk for some music. I had four large 12-inch speakers in my car's trunk that my dad and I had built a single wooden box for. It made for a really loud stereo system that was great for outdoor parties. The only problem was that running the stereo without the car running killed my car's battery. Once the battery died, and the music stopped a friend of mine came to me and offered to jump my car. I told him that I did not need a jump because I was not planning on driving anywhere that night. He insisted, though, and drove his car down to my party in the valley and jump started it.

During the peak of my party, I had well over one hundred guests. My parents also had around a hundred guests as well. At one point, my guests and I decided to throw many large dead pine tree branches onto our bomb fire. The fire rose to an immeasurable height, and it began to look like it was snowing when all the pine needle's ashes fell down on us. I stared into the fire, and for a minute or so I felt like I should walk into the flames.

It was as though some dark force was calling me. I had never felt suicidal before, and even today I would not say it was a suicidal tendency. It was more of a warm, comforting feeling like if I obeyed the feeling, I would enter into a warm place; but in reality, it would have burned me and given me an immense pain like I had never felt before. The screams of my guests are what brought me out of this strange trance that I had fallen into. My guests were throwing open cans of beer through the air while screaming that the beer was warm, and they had begun chanting "more beer, more beer, more beer!" Around this same time, my parents got word from some friends of theirs that they saw some of my guests stealing beer from their garage. My parent's also got word that there was a huge bomb fire back on their property, out of sight from the house down in the valley. My dad and a couple of his friends came down to my party and started questioning some of my guests where they had gotten their beer from.

My dad came up to me and pounded his finger into my chest and asked where his beer was. I told him I did not know. For fear that he would start a riot, my dad quit trying to find his beer and instead drove my car back up to our house. I followed him up to the house and asked him for my car keys back. He told me that they were his keys and then said to me that I was not driving anywhere that night. I had no intention of driving anyways and didn't really care where my keys had gone to.

Not long after my dad crashed our party most of my guests said they had to leave. One girl and her friend that I had driven to their house earlier that night before the party started, began asking if I could drive them home. I felt bad that they did not have a ride, so I went and asked my mother if she could drive them home. My mother told me I could drive them. It was obvious that she had not talked to my dad since he had driven my car up to the house. My mother asked if I was alright. I told her that I was. After all, I hadn't drunk very much that night compared to what I usually drank on the weekends, but I was beyond tired. I told the girl I would take them home. I drove just a little ways away from our home, then asked if one of the girls would drive. I wasn't supposed to drive past 11pm, and it was now beyond that time. So as I was accustomed to doing, I asked if anyone else would drive. The girl who was not old enough to drive yet, said she would drive. I gladly let her drive. Two other guys had joined us for the short ride.

We did not see any police cars on the way to her house, and there were rarely ever any police between her house and mine anyways. I figured that it was safe for me to drive the few miles back to my house. On the way back to my house we saw a lot of cars parked at another party. We decided to see who was at this party. The house that was hosting this party was on the water. We walked up to the house, but no one was in the house. On the way into the house, we had spotted a lot of alcohol in the garage. We decided that we should not stick around at this house, but instead, the three of us who were returning to my house each grabbed a case of beer from the garage. I figured I could take the beer to my parent's party and put it in their garage so that they would be glad I replaced the beer we had stolen. Once arriving back at my party, we discovered that someone had put our fire out and had invited what few remaining friends of mine were still there, to come up into our garage to make sure they were sober before driving home. All of the kids looked sober at this time. We put most of the beer we had stolen from the other party into my parent's garage, but some had fallen out of the cases and into my car's trunk. I began talking to my friends and making sure they were alright to drive home. I offered to let anyone who may have drunk too much to stay the night, but everyone assured me that they were not drunk and refused my offer.

I also knew that there was not very much beer at my party compared to how many people actually attended. I doubt there was even enough beer for each person to have had two beers. I know that I personally only had a couple of beers and a few shots. Everyone else probably didn't drink even as much as I did. With over one hundred guests, I would have had to have had over 10 cases of beer just for everyone to have had 2.4 beers each being there is only 24 beers in a case of beer. I think we only ever had around 7 cases at my party.

While we were in the garage is when a 17 year old boy, the same age I was at the time, approached me and asked me for a ride to his car. Since there was roughly 200 people total between my parent's party and mine, there were cars parked up to half a mile away from our house. I figured the boy was lazy and did not want to walk a half mile to his car, because when I told him to just walk, he told me it was too far to walk. I then noticed he had another boy with him who was also wanting a ride. I told him he could borrow my skateboard. He stated that there were too many of them to skateboard. I informed him that I had two skateboards and that they could borrow them both. He then told me that there were four of them, two boys and two girls that needed a ride.

By this time, it was around 1:00 am in the morning. I could barely think because of how little sleep I had had in the last two or three days. I asked where their car was located, and they told me it was at the park. There was a park about a half mile away from our house. I figured that cars had parked this far up and down our road because of how many people had attended our party. I agreed to give them a ride to this nearby park. The last thing I remember seeing at our house was one of the biggest guys in my graduating class arm wrestling my dad.

Chapter 5
"The Crash"

Life can change on a dime. Anyone who has suffered any sort of tragedy in life knows how much of a reality this is. One minute I remember saying I would take some kids that were stranded at my house to their car, the next minute I am standing in the middle of the road with my hands held out in front of me wondering where I was and how I had gotten there. My hands were extended in front of me at waist height, and my palms were facing to the night's sky. My entire body felt strangely numb, as though it was not awake.

There was a loud ringing in my ears that quickly faded away. I looked down at my feet and saw one of the boys I had agreed to take to their car laying there like he was sleeping. I wondered if he was alright or not, so I got down on my knees and checked both his pulse and whether he was breathing or not. He did have a pulse, but he was not breathing. I was just about to perform CPR on him when I heard a noise coming out of the road's ditch. I looked across the car's headlights and saw the other boy who was in the car approaching me. He was literally pulling hair out of his head while repeatedly saying, "I got to get out of here, I got to get out of here!" I told him not to run and that his friend needed our help, then told him to go get help. He began to run across the street when we both heard a male's voice come from the shadows saying that he had already called the police. The boy ran back to me and told me that one of the girls was down the street also on the road. I began to give his friend mouth to mouth resuscitation. The other boy then ran to where the girl in the road was and then came back to me. He said she was hurt pretty bad. I continued to give his friend the CPR, and then his friend began to shake a little. I thought he was going to start breathing, so I slightly lifted up his head, but to my terror, blood began to come out of his mouth.

I stood up and looked at my hands because they felt wet. I realized they were covered with blood. I wiped the blood on my pants to clean my hands off and that is when I saw one of the first medical responders arrive at the accident scene. I told the other guy to get the girl off the street so that no one would run her over. I had hopes that she would still be ok once she received medical attention. He dragged her off the road and then returned to where I was. It was not long before many other medical responders arrived at the scene of the accident. They quickly separated me from the other survivor and began asking us questions. They kept asking me where I was hurt. I told them that I was not hurt. They then informed me that I was hurt, but that I just did not know it because I was in shock. I thought that maybe they were right, after all, I did still feel quite numb.

Two guys then grabbed me by my arms and gently laid me on the ground. They began to ask me a few questions. They asked me what the date was. I didn't know because I never really cared about the date. They asked if I knew where I was. I didn't know exactly where I was. The last thing I knew, we were headed to a park that was located halfway between my house and the water. I could hear waves gently crashing on the shore, so I knew I was near the lake. I told them that I was on the peninsula, but exactly where, I was not sure. I thought I drove them to a park, but I never remember us leaving the park. The crashing waves I could hear let me know we had left the park at some point because we were beyond the park. Another question they asked me several times was if I was driving or if I knew who was driving. I told them I was not driving and that I did not know who was. I was pretty certain that I was not driving, but I didn't know who was.

The paramedics then began to cut my shirt and pants off. They saw a lot of blood on my legs and began wiping it off. I heard one paramedic keep asking where the cuts were, and another guy replied back that there were not any cuts. The blood was not my own. But there was too much blood to have just been from wiping my hands onto my pants. The only thing I can figure out was that I was kneeling in blood when I was trying to help save the one boy's life. The adrenalin of the accident was now wearing off, and I began to fall in and out of consciousness at this point. It didn't help that I had only had around two hours sleep in the last 48 plus hours. I don't remember a single moment of the ambulance ride to the hospital.

Once at the hospital, I recall being awakened several times by detectives and doctors. Each time I would wake up for a few minutes only to be bombarded with questions. The main question they kept asking me was if I knew who the driver was. I kept telling them that I did not. They asked me how many people were in the car and I told them that there were five people.

One time when I woke up for a short spell I remember I was lying in a small tunnel with a red light slowly going around my head. Another time I remember they had me stand up and hold onto something while they took x-rays of my chest. My dad came into my room a few times and told me he was at the hospital with my mom because she had stepped out of the garage wrong and broke her ankle. Our family did not have a telephone, and the police had no way to contact my family. My dad was at the hospital because of my mom's accident when he was asked if he had a son named Jash. All in all, it was a horrifying night. My mother was right, something bad did indeed happen.

Chapter 6
"The Next Day"

The next day I was again awakened several times by all sorts of people. I had a number of friends stop by to see me. Mostly I just wanted to sleep. I remember it being a little strange that a girl came to visit me who I hardly knew. She stuck around for quite some time. While she was in my hospital room is when I got a call from the other survivor of the crash. The first question I asked him was, "What happened?" That is when he told me I was the driver. This did not make sense to me. I was pretty sure that I was not the driver. I hadn't asked him who was driving, I just wanted to know what had happened. I was now very confused. I was telling the police and paramedics that I was not the driver and that I did not know who was. Now this guy just told me that I was the driver. I then asked him, "Didn't we stop at a park?"

He told me we did not. This confused me even more. I thought I remembered stopping at a park a short distance from my house and asking if someone else would drive, but had I just dreamt this? I then asked him a third and final question. I asked him if I had asked if someone else would drive. He did not answer my third and final question but instead hung his phone up on me. Why would he lie to me? Was he lying? Maybe I was confused. Maybe I had hit my head harder than I thought during the accident and we really just drove from my house to where the accident happened. But why did I think we stopped at a park and why couldn't I remember any of the car ride? I had only drunk a few beers that night and a couple of shots. I had drunk plenty more than that amount on other occasions and never had a memory problem like this. I continued to ponder and entertain the thought that maybe I was the driver, but I still couldn't believe it.

Once they released me from the hospital, I went to visit my mother in her hospital room. She rolled away from me and told me that I was in a lot of trouble. She then kept saying "those poor kids". She loved children and felt so bad for the ones who had died. I wasn't sure what she meant when she said I was in a lot of trouble. Was I in trouble even though I was not the driver, or did she think I was the driver? I didn't want to bother her with any questions because she was in a lot of pain and crying hysterically.

I remember being outdoors at the hospital with my dad and having him show me compassion. He told me he wished he could take my place and how bad he felt for me. Little did I know that this was just the beginning of one horrible nightmare that would last for decades.

I tried as hard as I could to remember what had happened the night before during the accident, but all I could get was a faint memory of stopping at a park and asking if someone else wanted to drive. It was as if I had gotten into the passenger's side of the car and fell asleep. You can't really remember anything while you are sleeping other than maybe your dreams.

Chapter 7
"Arrested and Jailed"

I was seventeen years old when the accident happened. The other survivor was the same age as I was, and the three who died were fifteen and sixteen years old. This was a horrible event for a couple of kids, seventeen years old to go through and even worse for the three that died and for those who loved them. It is very hard to just go back to a normal life after experiencing something like this, but it is what we were told to do by a therapist that my family went to see. He said that going back to work was what was best for us instead of just sitting around thinking about what happened. I went back to work, but I now had no car, and my social life came to a halt. I basically just surrounded myself with work and loud music. I began to buy a lot of music CDs. I tried to reach out to some of my friends, but very few wanted to really be around me. I was now the guy who always needed a ride and who no longer drank or did drugs.

It was probably a month or so before I heard any news from the police department. One of my close friends at the time worked with me at a local bakery. While he and I were alone at work one day, his dad who worked for the police department came into the bakery. He called his son to him and whispered something to him. His son ran off crying. He then turned to me and told me that it was time.

I asked if he was arresting me. He informed that he was not, but that he wanted to make sure the arresting officers treated me alright. It was only a few minutes later, when other officers showed up and began yelling at my friend's dad. They were mad that he was even there, and they were acting very overly aggressive. They did, however, treat me better than they probably would have if my friend's dad were not there to watch them.

I remember the ride to the police station and seeing the two arresting officers waving and nodding to a number of different undercover officers in other cars in nearby business parking lots. I guess there was a rumor that I might try and run when they came to arrest me, and they wanted to be ready to catch me if they had to.

I was taken to the county jail and told that I would be arraigned in a day or so. I woke up my first morning in jail with my head resting on my friend's mother's lap. She ran the county jail and was wife to the man who came to make sure they treated me well when they arrested me. Tears were falling from her face and landing onto mine. She was petting my hair while saying it would all be alright. A few days later I stood before a magistrate of the court. She came to the jail and was on the opposite side of a protection window from me. She informed me that I was charged with 3 felonies each carrying up to 15 years in prison and said she was setting my bond at $150,000. She then informed me that she had contemplated setting it lower, but instead decided to raise it higher and asked me what I thought about this? I told her that it did not matter if it was $15,000 or a $150,000, that I didn't have any money. I went back to my cell thinking I would be there for quite some time.

Physically, it was very hard the first few days being in jail because I was used to walking or riding my bike many miles a day. I usually got a ride into town with my dad to work, and then I would ride my bike 12 miles home. To now be locked up and confined in a small jail cell with two other guys was tormenting to a man who was used to being outside walking or riding a bike as often as I was. I felt like a caged bird who could no longer fly. One of the inmates in my cell said that he saw me moving around like I was riding a bike in my sleep a couple of times.

I remember one of my cellmates waking me up just in time to see a drunk driving commercial on the television. The guy in the commercial was talking in the picture area of a driver's license. He looked sort of like me, and the driver's license was cut in the top corner indicating that he got in trouble for drunk driving. What really got me suspicious was when I saw his birthdate on the driver's license and noticed that he had the same birthdate as mine; the exact same month, day and year. This was not a coincidence. And to have a cellmate, wake me up just in time to see it seemed strange also.

One inmate asked me how I felt about being in jail during the summer when there was so much to do. I told him it didn't bother me. He told me that I could be locked up for a long time. This didn't bother me either. What really bothered me was the fact that they charged me and were going to try me for a crime I was sure I did not commit. This was when I began to have some serious doubts about my innocence. Maybe I really was the driver? Would the police and district attorney really charge and arrest me if I was not the driver? I was wondering if there was something they knew that I did not know.

After 10 days of being locked up, I was called out of my jail cell to visit with my court-appointed attorney. He informed me that my parents worked out some sort of deal with the district prosecutor/attorney and that I was being released on a $150,000 bond. My parent's put up their $23,000 of the equity they had in their home, and the rest of the bond was a personal recognizance bond. I was told that if I did not do all that they required or tried to leave the town, my parents would lose their house, and I would have to pay back the rest of the money to meet the $150,000 requirement. I was then told what all of my bond conditions were. I had to show up at the police station each and every morning 365 days a year and take a breathalyzer to prove that I was not drinking any alcohol. I was to maintain full-time employment or go to school full time. I had to be home by 10:00 pm each night. I could not drive any motorized vehicle. Which included a moped, boat, or tractor. I was also not allowed to use any illegal drugs. Having so many restictions on my life was a big surprise to me. I was a man who was supposedly innocent until proven guilty, yet my entire life was now being controlled by the court system. I thought to myself, at least I am sort of free, instead of locked in a cell.

As the days went on, I found out that being on a bond was not very fun at all. My parents would flip out if I pushed the limit and got home just a few minutes before my 10pm curfew. They were under the impression that they would lose the new house that they had just finished building if I was even one minute late. One night a friend of mine was waiting for his dad to get home so he could give me a ride home with his dad's car. When his dad had not arrived home in time, he scrummaged through his house and found some motorcycle keys and had me jump on the back of a motorcycle. We only had a few minutes to cover a lot of miles to my house. I think he drove that motorcycle over a hundred miles an hour. It then began to rain out, and we slid sideways around one corner, but somehow managed to stay upright. I thought I was going to die that day just so I could get home by 10:00 at night.

The hardest part of my bond conditions was having to be at the police station every single day in the early morning hours to take a breathalyzer. I remember getting to the police station just in time a few times. A couple of times, the nice lady that ran the breathalyzer testing room, even stayed open for a few extra minutes knowing I was probably just running late. During the work week, I would go to work, work a few hours, punch out of work, then walk or ride my bike down to the police station to take a breathalyzer. This used to anger me because I basically had to take an hour off work, which meant I missed out on six hours of overtime pay each week, then to even make it costlier to me, I had to pay for the breathalyzers that I was being forced to take each day. I basically no longer felt like I was living in a free country, but rather in a police state, or worse, a communist country. How could they control my life so much when I was innocent, or at the least, innocent until proven guilty? It didn't make sense that they could force me to do something each day and then on top of that, make me pay for it. And I can't stress how inconvenient it is to have to report to the police station every single day of the year between two early morning hours.

For a brief amount of time, a woman started working at the bakery I was working at. She insisted on driving me down to the police station to take my breathalyzers. One day when she brought me back to work, she hit the car brakes harder than usual. A full can of beer rolled out from under the seat I was sitting in and hit me in the heel of my right foot. She told me I could take it with me, that I wouldn't have another breathalyzer for 24 hours. I told her thanks, but no thanks. At the time it did not dawn on me that she worked for the police, but when I told my boss about the incident, he told me she was probably a cop. This suddenly made complete sense to me. She had taken me out to a small town a week or so earlier and told me she had a place I could get a job and make more money than I was making. While waiting for an interview, a guy came into the waiting room and told me I could help myself to the beer that was in the refrigerator. He told me not to worry about the women that she was cool with me drinking.

This should have been enough to let me know that she was a police officer. She also always wore yellow tinted sunglasses that looked like they were used for shooting a gun. It was hard to believe that my town's police station would have someone work undercover to keep an eye on me and try to get me to violate my bond by drinking. It wasn't like I was a big-time drug dealer or crime boss of some sort. And why would they try to get me to violate my bond? The answer to that question became clear to me later in my life.

Chapter 8
"Pretrial"

My parents were charged with the crime of contributing alcohol to minors. Some friends of mine and I stole beer from my parents the night of the party, my parents were now being charged with a crime because of this. It was a misdemeanor crime that held up to 90 days in the county jail. Besides being charged with 3 accounts of OUIL (Operating Under Intoxicating Liquor) Causing Death, which carried up to 15 years in prison for each charge, I also was charged with contributing alcohol to minors. This misdemeanor crime was the only crime I was truly guilty of, but regardless of this truth, I had to attend a pretrial so that the court could determine if they would move forward with the 3 felony crimes I was charged with as well.

At my pretrial is when I first discovered just how slow and messed up the entire judicial system was, and probably still is. My attorney told me that the district attorney was going to present evidence to support the crimes I was charged with. I looked forward to this because as far as I knew, the only evidence they had was the other survivor's testimony. I didn't think they could charge someone on just one person's word. What if that person is lying? It was really his word against mine. I thought the entire pretrial was going to take up to ten minutes. I figured they would put the other survivor on the stand, cross examine him, declare that it was his word against mine, and rule that there was not sufficient evidence to move forward.

Boy was I wrong! It seemed more like a drunk driving commercial than anything else. They went into great detail on how the kids died from certain injuries that they sustained. They talked about how dangerous drunk driving was, and they went on and on about how I had been drinking that night and that I was just slightly over the drunk driving level and also went into fine details about how the car crashed into the trees and which way it spun and landed.

I could not believe that the only evidence they had pointing to me as the driver was the testimony of one unreliable person who I thought was probably the driver himself. What about fingerprints, what about injuries sustained during the crash that placed the car's occupants in certain seats, what about me taking the stand to defend myself. I am not certain if it is normal for a person to defend themselves at a pretrial or not, but it seems more effort in discovering the truth and more evidence should be presented then just one person pointing their finger at someone and accusing them of committing a crime. Why even have a pretrial if no genuine evidence is required? I saw it all as just part of being a show and a way to try and tell kids they should not drink and drive then an actual productive step in our judicial system. I'm pretty sure that there was some amateur film crew filming the pre-trial to teach kids not to drink and drive. It seemed that everyone was catering to the camera more so than focusing on whether there was any substantial evidence backing up the charges against me.

The pretrial itself was months after the accident and in my eyes, was just a waste of time. Now I was told that the trial would not begin for many more months. If nothing else came from the pretrial, I got a first impression of how inadequate the judicial system is, and I was also given an idea of what little evidence there actually was against me; just one man's word.

Chapter 9
"The Police Report & The Star Witness's Inconsistent Statements to the Police"

I can't remember if it was before or after the pretrial that I tried to go and see the District Attorney to ask him why he thought I was the driver. He stopped me in the lobby of the building that his office was in and told me that he could not meet with me; that any conversations between him and I had to go through my attorney.

I went to my attorney and asked him what other evidence the district attorney (DA) was relying on besides the one guy's testimony. My attorney said he did not know and then handed me a police report that was hundreds of pages long. I read through the entire police report and discovered that there was not any evidence that pointed towards me as being the driver. And what was even far more interesting to me, was that the star witness the DA was relying entirely on had changed his story four times. This was proof he was lying.

#1. When first asked, who was driving the car, the other survivor said that there was a sixth person in the car and that he thinks they were driving but that they fled the accident scene. This is why the police asked me how many people were in the car when they questioned me in the hospital. I told them that there were only five people in the car.

#2. Later on, when the police asked the other survivor a second time about who was driving the car, he told them that he did not know who was driving.

#3. The police then informed him that they wanted to take a blood sample from him to test his alcohol level in case he was the driver, he changed his story a third time and told them that he thinks I was the driver but that he was not sure at this time.

#4. This was when some of the pieces of the puzzle began to really come together. Come to find out, it wasn't until his fourth statement to the police that he really pointed the finger at me. His fourth statement was not until he called me in the hospital and told me I was the driver. I began to question him during our phone conversation, but he cut the phone conversation short and hung up on me. Then he turned to a police sergeant who was by his side when he called me and told him that I was the driver.

Unknown to me, this police sergeant's daughter was standing by my side in the hospital room when I received this call from him. It was the girl I barely knew who hung out at the hospital longer than anyone else. This father and daughter eavesdropping team listened to both sides of our phone conversation. This fourth statement from this other survivor was contradicted by his first three statements made to the police only a few hours prior.

The rest of the police report mainly consisted of just interviews with the hundreds of people who had attended either my parents' party or my party. The police interviewed the people to see if they knew anything, like whether they saw me drinking, how much they saw me drink and whether they knew if I was driving the car or not. One cousin of mine said she saw us leave the party in my car before the motorcycle accident happened and before my mother broke her ankle. At the time, I did not know how relevant this information was.

Chapter 10
"Parents Jailed"

My parents had a court date coming up for the contributing alcohol to minor charges that they were charged with. I felt like they needed to fight the charges because they were being charged because some friends and I stole beer from them. It wasn't like my parents were down at my party handing out cans of beer to my guests, which was actually the opposite of the truth. My dad came down to my party to try and get his beer back, not give it away.

But my parents were told that with them taking some of the blame, it would take some of the attention away from me and that I probably would not get punished as severly if they did not fight their charges, but rather just pleaded no contest to their charges.

The attorney, my parents, hired told them that they would not both go to jail at the same time, that because they had two teenage sons, the judge would have one of them serve their sentence and once they finished theirs, then the other could go in and serve their sentence. Their attorney also told them that they would probably get work release and be able to keep their jobs, and that they would only have to stay in jail at night. My parents did not trust their attorney, so they sold their boat, tractor, and my dad's truck and stashed the money in case they did have to each spend 90 days in jail and lose their jobs. My mom was pretty sure she would lose her job if she had to serve 90 days in jail. My dad figured he would still have his.

The day came for my parents to stand before the judge. The judge told them they were both being sentenced to 90 days in jail, the maximum amount of time he could give them. Then he said that they were both to begin their 90-day sentence immediately, and that they would not get work release. My mom often lives by the saying, "Expect the worst, but hope for the best." They had hoped the judge would do what their attorney was telling them would happen, but they prepared for the worst possible outcome. The worst possible outcome is what happened.

I had just turned 18 years old a few months prior to my parents being sent away to jail. My younger brother was only 16 years old. I suddenly became his legal guardian. Most people at eighteen years old are not ready to live on their own in a good-sized house, much less prepared to take care of a sixteen-year-old. I was still working full time at a bakery during the day, and taking college classes at night. I had to be at the bakery early in the morning, which meant I would go to bed early. But my brother, on the other hand, was still in high school, and my friends that were already graduated from high school that were hanging around our house, didn't have to go to bed early. My parent's house had become more or less a party house for teenagers. I was either away from home or asleep most of the time, but when I did stay up or not have to be to work or school, it was a wild living environment.

One day I woke up and discovered that two of our house's front windows were broken out. Another night when I woke up early to go to work, the partiers had thrown liquid laundry detergent, all over the walls and themselves and had a black light on, that made the liquid glow a strange color. For the most part, I was not that upset with what was going on, but then the parties became more and more frequent, and the teenagers began playing with an Ouija board.

One night after some of the teenagers played with the Ouija board they decided to go to a church up the road from my house and steal from it. While one guy was taking altar wine from a cupboard, a statue fell onto him and knocked him out. He thought his friend had pushed it over onto him, but his friend says he did not touch the statue. I think one could conclude that it was a sign that God did not like what they were doing.

I didn't like the way some of the people who were beginning to act who were playing with the Ouija board, and I was starting to not like the thing itself. I found it unexplainable and creepy. The board would answer questions I asked it that no one else in the group could possibly know. I thought that maybe I unconsciously pushed the eyepiece to answer the questions, so I experimented with it by not even touching the eyepiece and let only other people touch it. I asked a question that no one could know, and it still answered the question correctly. I could feel a strange chill anytime I would be staring at it, and it began to answer my question, even when I was not touching any part of it. It felt like the game would connect with me. If I looked away from the board and took my mind off of it, I would feel a disconnection, and it would stop answering my question, even if it had already written out half of a word to answer my question. It would just start going in circles until I would look at it again and reconnect with it.

I really didn't like when the board would go evil and start saying things like "You are all going to die!" The whole thing really started to bother me. One day when I went to visit my parents in jail, I told them about the Ouija board. They told me to get rid of it, that it was against our religion. I asked them what religion we were of. They said they did not know, but that it did not consist of Ouija boards.

A friend of mine who refused to touch the board told me I needed to burn the board. He then said to me that he tried to destroy one that he and his brother used to have and that it just kept mysteriously coming back until they burned it. He said his house got possessed by it and that they had to have a couple guys perform an exorcism on his house. After hearing my friend's story, I took a knife and scratched "God help us" into the board, poured some gasoline onto it, and burned it to a crisp, just to be safe. I knew so little about God and religion. I had a Bible that someone gave me when I was in the county jail for the ten days, but had not read any of it. A guy who had basically moved into my house while my parents were locked up asked me if I talked to God when he saw the Bible I had. I lied and told him that I talked to God all of the time, to make a joke out of our conversation. He seemed very surprised at my answer. I then said, "God just never talks back." We both laughed at this. He told me he had a grandmother who talks to God, which I thought was strange.

While my parents were locked up, I paid their bills. I mostly used the money they had saved up from selling some of their things, but I remember that it ran out fairly quickly and I had to make a payment or two for them. I was shocked at how much their bills were. Being on my own for nearly three months at age 18 was another big eye opener in my life.

When the day came for my parents to be released, I was relieved. They returned home to discover several freeloaders who had moved into our house. My parents went through their entire house looking for any drug paraphernalia. To my surprise, my dad found some hidden under the kitchen sink. I think he also found some elsewhere also. My parents told everyone who had moved in that they had to get out. I was so glad they were home and had taken back control of the house.

Chapter 11
"Charges Dropped"

One day I was contacted by my attorney who told me he had some good news for me. I went to his office, and he told me that the judge had dropped the charges against me. For a brief moment, I thought that they had all seen the light and now knew I was innocent and that the system was actually not broken. But then I was disappointed when I was informed that the reason the charges were dropped was that the judge had ruled that the law I was charged with was unconstitutional. My attorney told me that I could still be charged with a different crime or that the DA may appeal the judge's decision but that for now, it was a win.

My attorney loved seeing his face on the front page of the local newspaper. I, on the other hand, could not stand it. I was in the paper countless of times. Each time the article or local news station talked about me, they would say that I was the driver of the car. I thought it was illegal to say false things like this in a paper. I felt that the paper could get into trouble for lying about me. I said something to a few people, and the next thing I knew, the media started to say that I was "allegedly" the driver of the car, or say things like, "according to the police", I was the driver. I figured this was the media's way of getting around not getting in trouble for lying about me. But it was not long before the media started stating it as a fact again. The charges being dropped was a big deal. I thought this also meant that I could go back to a normal life. My attorney met with me again a short time later and said that the DA was appealing the judge's decision and that this meant I was still to remain on bond. I was however taken off of my daily breathalyzers.

At one point I had to go and meet with the Secretary of State regarding my driver's license. When I arrived for my hearing, I was taken off guard when there were two other people in the office besides me and the hearings investigator, one of which was a police officer in uniform and another was a detective in a suit and tie. The hearings investigator told me that because I got charged with a drunk driving causing death charge, he had to have a hearing to determine how I should be punished by his office. I asked him and the police why they thought I was the driver.

My question caused the police officer and detective to instantly get mad and they told the investigator that they believed that I was the driver. They didn't present any evidence; they just told him that it was their belief. They then turned towards me and told me to "shut up", that I should not say anything because I did not have an attorney present. They took over the meeting and silenced me with their authority and overbearingness. The guy who was truely the one in control had me go wait out in the lobby and then talked to the them privately. A short time later the police officer and detective left his office, and he called me back in. They gave me a stern, mean look as they left. The hearings investigator was very kind and gentle. I think he could sense that something was wrong. He told me he was taking my license away for one year and told me that if I ever needed to talk to someone, I could contact him.

Chapter 12
"Running from the Law"

While I was still working at the bakery, a co-worker convinced me that I should go back to smoking marijuana for just a little while. I decided that I would take his advice and do it for a couple of weeks. I told myself that I would quit on the last day of March. A few days before I was going to quit, I won a small jackpot playing the lotto. I told a guy at college how much I had won, and he said he could get me a good size bag of marijuana for that amount. I had never bought as much marijuana as he was suggesting I should buy, and I thought it would be a nice treat. April first came a few days later, and I suddenly remembered that it was the day I was going to go back clean. I made a joke out of it and said to myself, "April Fools," and decided that I was not going to quit just yet. But the joke was on me.

Later that day my boss fired me because he said someone smelled me smoking marijuana in the bathroom. The boss then told me he thought that the two guys he had recently hired were also cops. It suddenly made sense why these two guys knew my friend whose dad was an undercover cop pretty well. My friend told me that they were the same two guys who had done the exorcism on his house when his house had gotten possessed from playing with a Ouija board.

I thought my boss was kidding when he said I was fired and I laughed. I couldn't believe he would fire me for smoking marijuana when he smoked more marijuana than anyone I had ever met. He told me he was not kidding and that is when he told me he thought the two new guys he had hired worked for the police. This made me now take him seriously, it also made me afraid, for I had just violated two of my bond conditions.

Two of my bond conditions were that I was supposed to maintain full-time employment, and I was not supposed to use any illegal drugs. I was afraid that my parents would lose their house because I violated my bond, so I ran to a bigger city called Grand Rapids, which was about two and a half hours south of my town. I went to this other city so that I could hide from the police while I flushed the evidence of drugs out of my body. To do this, I just needed a few days, some specific type of pills, and I would need to consume a lot of water.

I rented a hotel room in Grand Rapids and was bored out of my mind in no time. I walked to a local mall and socialized with a few girls there my age. Later that evening I met another young woman at a restaurant, and she said I should meet her and some of her friends at a club near my hotel the next night. I told her that sounded like fun and that I would see her there.

The next day I walked to a nearby college and found myself in one of its' residential dorms. While walking through the dorm, I was very excited. It seemed there was nothing but girls my age. I saw no boys. What excited me the most was that some of these young women were wearing nothing but their undergarments. One of the young ladies stopped me and asked how I got into their dorm? I wasn't sure what she was asking me, so with half a grin on my face, I told her I had walked. She didn't think my answer was very funny and then told me that I was in an all girl's Christian dorm and then repeated her original question. She then also asked how I got by the woman at the front desk. Fear immediately struck my heart, and I quickly fled out of the dorm. The last thing I needed was someone calling the police on me. I still had a pocket full of marijuana, and I was on the run from the law. What really made me believe my boss was right about his two new employees being undercover cops, was that my boss, and the rest of his employees, were all questioned by the police shortly after he fired me. Somehow the police knew I was fired almost immediately after it happened.

While I was trying to leave the college campus as fast as I could without drawing attention to myself, I was stopped by another young woman outside who asked if I was coming to watch the speaker that was speaking at their school that night. She was pointing at a building not far from us indicating that that was where he was speaking at. For a moment, I considered attending the assembly with her, she had even held out a hand as if she would be my date, but then fear struck my heart again when I began to think about how the girls in the dorm may have called the police on me. I told her that I did not go to this school and didn't think I could go.

She said she would go in and ask if I was allowed, but I politely thanked her and told I her that I had to be going. The girl looked like she may have been an angel, and I so badly wish I could have joined her, but instead, I walked away sorrowful and full of fear. I don't know if she prayed for me that evening or if one of the girls in the dorm did, but I believe someone must have because of what happened the next day.

Chapter 13
"Born Again"

On the way back to my hotel from the college, I decided to look for the nightclub that I was invited to by the women I met at the restaurant. I walked up and down the road a few times by where she said the nightclub was at, but I didn't see it anywhere, so I called it a night and went back to my hotel room.

The next day I decided I would go to the mall again. When I got to the mall's parking lot, I noticed that there were not any cars in the lot. I thought this was strange being that the mall should have been open at this time. As I began to walk across the parking lot to investigate why no one was there, I noticed that there was a very large banner sign hanging above the mall's doors.

Once I was close enough to read the sign I saw that it said, "Have a Happy Easter!" That is just great, I thought to myself. All I knew about Easter was chocolate Easter bunnies, colored eggs, and that nothing in town would be open. I started walking back to my hotel room with my head hung low in despair. I believed this was going to be the most boring day of my life. All I kept thinking about was how I was so stupid for doing drugs again and was deeply afraid that my parents were going to lose their house, and that I was about to be thrown into jail for a very long time. I felt so burdened that I could literally feel a heavy weight on my shoulders. I was 18 years old and felt like life was harder and far more unfair than it was supposed to be. While heading back to my hotel from the mall, I noticed a number of people going into a building I was walking by. These people looked like they were all dressed up, for a wedding or something. I decided I would go look in through the building's doors windows.

If there was a wedding reception or some sort of party happening, there was bound to be alcohol at it. Getting drunk at this point in my life was very appealing. It would help me get my mind off of what was going on in my life. It would get my mind off of why I was in this big strange city to begin with.

I was planning on just saying I was a friend of John's if anyone asked who invited me. The odds were in my favor that there would be a John in attendance, being that it is such a common name. When I looked through the windows, I realized that it was not a wedding reception at all. I wasn't sure what it was, but I didn't see any alcohol there, and fear started to take over my heart again, so I began to walk away very quickly.

I didn't make it very far when a guy came running out after me. He shouted out, "Brother, brother, come in; the Lord has sent you." What? What was this guy talking about? No one had sent me. Part of me really wanted to just keep walking away, but another part of me was saying, "What else do you have to do?" I was torn between two thoughts. Should I accept the guy's invitation to go in, or go back to my hotel room? While I was trying to decide, the guy came out to me and put his hand on my shoulder and again invited me to come inside.

Hesitantly, I walked into the building, and the guy's face lit up as I did so. He took me into an auditorium and showed me a seat. I sat there for a few minutes looking around. I noticed that everyone in the building were African Americans. Immediately a voice in my heart said, "You have to get out of here, you have to get out of here right now!" I also kept hearing the word "racism" repeatedly in my head, and something telling me that I was not welcomed there because I was white. It was as though something was yelling in my ear, "you are not welcome here!". Just when I was about to get up and leave the building, a woman sat down next to me whose skin was as dark as the night's sky. She took one look at me and said, "Welcome, welcome," while patting me on my left leg.

I could not believe what just happened. I suddenly felt very welcome in that place, so I decided to stay. Was this lady a real person, or was she an angel? To this day I do not know, and this was just the beginning. Not long after this seriously dark-skinned, kind and gentle lady patted me on the lap, a guy came out on the stage and began fervently preaching and a band began to play all sorts of musical instruments. There were guitars, drums, and microphones. This did not seem like a church to me at all. I was only ever used to bells and harps at a church. The man was preaching with fervent heat! And more than preaching. One of the first things I remember him screaming out of his mouth was, "Are you running from the law?" Talk about paranoia! I suddenly thought that the police from my city had found me and were orchestrating this whole event just for their amusement. I started looking around expecting to see the police coming down the aisles with handcuffs in hand to arrest me.

After looking around for a little while, I looked back up to the preacher who was still fervently preaching. He looked my way and then yelled out, "Are you looking for alcohol?" What? My mind could not comprehend what was happening. No one could have possibly known that I approached this building in hopes that there was alcohol being served in it.

In my heart, I asked myself how this could all be possible. That is when it was as if the preacher answered a question I had only asked myself in my mind. He yelled out, "It is God! God knows everything about you!" Then he gave an invitation to anyone who has heard from God that night to come up and get saved. I thought I was the only one who had heard from God and was way too afraid to be the only one to walk up to the stage to get saved. I wasn't even sure what he had meant when he had said get saved. I hadn't heard much of his sermon because I was distracted from looking around wondering if the police had set this whole event up. I do remember that the preacher had talked about how when a demon gets cast out of a person, the demon runs around looking for a place to stay and when he can't find a place, he comes back to the person he was cast from and brings seven other demons with him and makes himself at home again and the person is worse off than they were to begin with. I felt this was all true in my heart because

I had quit smoking marijuana for 10 months, and I only intended on going back for a few weeks, but now my life was more of a mess than it ever was before. I heard the preacher calling for more people to come up to the stage to be set free and to be saved. There were probably a hundred people who had responded to his first invitation. Now I saw about another fifty-people going up to his second invitation. Apparently, I was not the only person God was speaking to that evening.

Once I truly realized that it was God who had orchestrated this entire event, and not the police from my puny little town, I began to cry. I tried to hide my tears by putting on sunglasses, and by wiping my tears away using my shoulder. Two people then came to me and told me to come with them. They took me by the arms and basically carried me out of the sanctuary because of how weak my knees had suddenly become. After leaving the sanctuary, they lead me up some steps on the other side of the lobby. While going up the steps, I removed my sunglasses. My eyes were not adjusted to the bright lights in the lobby and staircase due to how dim the auditorium was and how dark my sunglasses were. I don't know if the tears had something to do with it as well, as if they may have been magnifying the brighter light, but it was so blinding, it was as if I was walking up into heaven itself.

After we reached the top of the steps, we then entered a classroom of some sort. The first thing I saw in this room was a woman who was hunched over. One guy was holding her up by her waist, while another guy had one of his hands placed on her forehead. She was screaming at the top of her lungs. I didn't know what to do. Part of me wanted to run away, but another part of me wanted to help her. It didn't look like the two guys were hurting her, but I couldn't figure out why she was yelling. The guy who had a hand on her forehead kept shouting out some sort of commands.

One of the guys who had taken me upstairs was walking toward me with one of his hands held up as though he was going to put it on my forehead. I kept walking backward until I was stuck in a corner of the room. He kept trying to ask me a question, but I could not hear him because I was too distracted by the woman they were giving an exorcism to. I kept trying to look around the guy to see the women, but the guy kept stepping in front of me blocking my view of her. The woman was still screaming loud when the guy decided he was going to scream out the question he had tried asking me a couple of times already. Just as he screamed out, "Do you know Jesus?" the woman had quit screaming. It was now dead silent in the room. I responded to the guy's question with one word, "no." "Well let me tell you about him," said the guy with a smile now on his face. He calmly began to tell me all about Jesus. He told me how Jesus came to the earth and was born of a virgin, and how Jesus had lived a perfect life and then was crucified for our sins. He then explained how if I put my trust in Jesus, I will live forever in heaven. He asked me if I wanted to do this. I immediately said, "yes".

The man then told me to pray with him, to repeat what he prays. Later I had discovered that he basically led me through the sinner's prayer. All I remembered at the time was saying my name and something about being sorry for my sins, then confessing that I believe Jesus died and then rose from the dead, and then at the end of the prayer, I asked Jesus Christ to be my Lord and Savior. Just as I said the words, "Jesus Christ, be my Lord and Savior," I felt a release. It was as if a thousand pounds had been taken off my shoulders. My heart felt so light and free from life's burdens. The man told me to look up, so I did. He said to me that even though I could not see it, thousands of angels were celebrating at that very moment. In my heart, I felt that what he was saying was true. I began to feel so happy that I started to cry. This was a totally new experience, for I had never cried tears of joy in my life before that day.

The guy then asked me if I had a problem with drugs. Instantly, I became very paranoid again and had a thought that maybe he was working with the police or maybe the police would wind up questioning him. I quickly told the guy that I did not have a problem with drugs. He then asked if I had a problem with smoking cigarettes. I thought to myself, "how does he know?" It was just like how the preacher was saying things a few minutes earlier that no one could know. No one knew I was out looking for alcohol and how does he know I do drugs and have a problem with smoking cigarettes? Just then, he answered the question I was thinking in my mind. He told me that he knew because he could smell them on me and even see the pack of cigarettes in my front shirt pocket. It was as if both him and the preacher were reading my mind.

The guy then told me to ask Jesus to help me quit smoking. I told him I can't do that because Jesus is dead. "Don't go back on your faith now brother," said the guy. "You just confessed in that prayer you prayed with me that you believe Jesus died, but you also confessed that you believe he rose from the dead. That is what this day is all about. Today is Easter Sunday, the day Jesus rose from the dead."

I still thought the guy might be pulling my leg. I had never really talked to someone that I could not see before. If I was going to be the butt of a joke, I was going to laugh with him. So really sarcastically I looked up at the ceiling and shouted out, "Jesus Christ, help me quit smoking!" I looked back at the guy thinking he was going to tell me something about how it doesn't really work that way and we would then laugh at how gullible I was, but instead, the guy just smiled at me and said, "welcome to the family brother." He told me he had asked Jesus to help him quit smoking10 years ago and has not smoked a cigarette since that day. Then he asked if I was from the area? I informed him that I was not. He then told me that my town needed Jesus also. He then patted me on the back and led me out of the building. What a strange experience. I went back to my hotel room trying to soak it all in and then fell asleep with the greatest peace of mind I had ever had.

Chapter 14
"The Following Days"

The next day I woke up with a severe pain in my throat. I looked over at my pack of cigarettes on my nightstand, and instead of wanting my first morning cigarette, I didn't want to touch them. I just kept hearing myself yelling out sarcastically, "Jesus Christ, help me quit smoking!" It kept repeating in my mind like a skipping record, over and over again. I had woken up with a severe case of strep throat. I was so amazed by what was happening. This was an answer to my prayer. I still felt so at peace. The heavy burden I took downstate with me was gone. I called my parents up and asked them to come get me. I was pretty sure that I had the drugs washed out of my system and I couldn't wait to tell my parents what had happened.

As far as my parents were concerned, they thought they could still lose their house because of the violation of my bond. Even though there were no drugs in my system, I still did not have a full-time job. I think it is strange that the court system can force a person to work a full-time job, especially since I was charged with a crime I did not commit. Even if I had committed the crime, I was not tried for it yet. Our country has the motto, "Innocent until proven guilty," but it sure felt like they were already treating me like I was guilty by how controlling over my life they were being. The car ride back to our city is one I will never forget. I was so excited about what had happened. It was still hard to comprehend that I had had a run in with God himself. It was because of the way that the preacher had said things only I knew about in my heart, that I was convinced it was God talking to me through this preacher. I told my parents about the whole experience and about how at the end of the night I accepted Jesus Christ as my Lord and Savior. My parents instantly took offense and asked me what religion it was? I told them I did not know.

They tried to tell me that we had a certain religion, but we had not gone to church in quite some time. They then asked me if I wanted to serve a God who makes me sick. I told them that I was sick because I had asked God to help me and this was his way of helping me. My parents now seemed even a bit angrier than they were when they first picked me up. I, on the other hand, was still so at peace and filled with overwhelming joy. I sat in the back seat of our vehicle with a big smile on my face.

I looked out a side window as we drove away from the hotel I was staying at. To my surprise, I saw the nightclub I was supposed to meet the women and her friends at that I had met my first night in that city. I thought it was strange that it was so easy to spot now, but that when I looked for it the other night, I could not find it. I now wonder if I was blinded to it by God himself. When I had intently looked for it, I could not find it, but now when I wasn't even trying to look for it, I saw it. If I had hooked up with that woman in the red dress and her friends that night, I might have never wound up getting saved. I have heard that the devil often does not come to us men sporting horns and carrying a pitchfork. He is far more effective when he comes to us wearing a red dress.

After driving for a half hour or so, my dad asked my mom if she was hungry. In an angry tone of voice, she said "No." In the exact opposite, excited type of voice, I said, "I am!" This was the last straw with my mother. She is usually a peaceful, kind and loving person, but when you are angry and scared, it is hard to be around people who are extremely happy, and she lost control. She grabbed an open pack of fig newton cookies and threw them at me while yelling out, "EAT THESE!" Many of them fell onto the floor. Then she grabbed a tennis shoe and threw that at me as well. The strange thing is, the joy I had seemed to only increase at this point. I started to pick up the cookies from the floor of our Ford Bronco and eat them. They tasted like the best thing in the world. Because of the peace and joy flooding my heart, mind, and soul, I just knew everything was going to be ok. This peace and security I was experiencing were supernatural.

The day I got saved (born again) was April 3rd. The car accident happened May 23rd the year before. I had been on bond for nearly a year at this point. I had never heard of someone waiting to go to court for this long, little did I know this was only the beginning of my experience with the court system, and it was also, just the beginning of my encounters with God.

I found a new job within no time as a busboy at a restaurant within walking distance of my house. I liked my new job. It was a change of pace for me. I had worked at a restaurant before, but this one was different. I liked working with the public versus working at a small bakery where I only saw the same few people each day. The people I worked for also seemed to like me. I always went out of my way to help the waiters and waitresses. Many of the wait staff were telling me I should move up to be a waiter myself, but that job looked much more stressful than mine, so I declined.

A guy at my new job started throwing some parties at a house just down the road from my house. He was inviting everyone from work. After hearing from numerous workers how much fun they had at his last party, I felt very left out. I wanted to stay away from the drugs and alcohol that were at parties like this, but being that most of our co-workers were beautiful women, I wanted so badly to attend one of his parties.

After working at this new job for only around a month, and exactly one year after the accident, I got talked into going to my co-worker's next party. He could tell I wanted to attend and easily talked me into going. I was eighteen at this time and really wanted a girlfriend. It seemed all the women from work were going to this party, and after being asked a few times, I gave in and said I would go. I told myself I would not do any drugs or drink; I was just going to hopefully woo one of these beautiful women into falling in love with me. I was still a virgin at this time and had so many dreams of falling in love and getting married.

My biggest dream was to become a young father. My mother was still a teenager when she had me, and my dad was not much older than her. I loved having young parents. I felt they were young enough to still do all the fun stuff in life, like hiking, fishing, boating, camping, etc. So, I went to this party hoping I would find a future wife. Instead, the darkness got the best of me.

Chapter 15
"Another Party"

When I first arrived at the party, hardly any of the women from my work were there yet. Most of them were still working. Instead, there were numerous men I had never met before just standing around drinking. One guy told me I could drink from the keg they had If I paid him $5.00. I told him thanks, but no thanks, because I wasn't drinking. Another guy then approached me and told me everyone was drinking, that that was the reason we were all there and told me I should drink too. I told him that I was ok, that I was there to hang out and that I didn't have five dollars anyway to pay for the beer. I was embarrassed to tell him my hopes of finding a woman to fall in love with and marry.

It wasn't long before a third guy came up to me and gave me a red plastic cup and told me I didn't have to pay, but I had to drink with them. I had never had so much pressure like that to drink before. The guy even helped me hold my cup up to the keg by holding my hand and pulling it forward, while another guy with an evil looking grin pumped the keg. I told the guy I couldn't drink, that there was a cop at the party. I knew that one of the guys had just graduated from a police training program. They said that he was not a cop, that he had only gotten a job at the local jail as a jail officer. Besides that, they said that he had already drunk a lot and was himself going to break the law by driving home later. They then told me that I only lived down the street and that I was just skateboarding home, that it was not as if I was going to break the law like the jail officer was going to. By this time, I had three guys all around me trying to get me to drink. I gave in to their pressure and lifted the cup of beer to my lips.

A couple sips into my beer, suddenly, standing right next to me, was my ex-probation officer. He said, "Hi Jash, remember me?" I told him I did remember him. He then asked what I was doing. I tried to explain to him that I didn't want to drink but he didn't want to hear about it. I skateboarded home as fast as I could and told my mother what had happened. My mother drove me back to the party and told me I had to get out of this trouble, but it was too late. The probation officer had already left to go home to fill out a report. The guy who threw the party came running up to me and gave me a big fat kiss right on the lips and told me "Thank You!" I wasn't sure what he meant. I didn't know why he had thanked me. All I knew was that I had never been kissed by a guy before and I did not like it at all. It wasn't until months later that I found out that this guy was in trouble with the law himself and that by getting me in trouble, it got him out of trouble.

I stayed at the party the rest of the night. I did meet a woman later that night that I thought I would marry. She took me into the fully blossoming cherry orchard and made love to me. I was 18, and she was 25, but she seemed to be very nice. Something did not seem right though. And even though a part of me loved the feeling of making love for my first time, another part of me felt like it was dying. I felt very dirty on the inside. I asked the woman if she might now be pregnant, but she then told me with a tear in her eye that she was barren. I had never heard the word barren before and asked her what it meant. She told me that being barren means a person cannot get pregnant. She also said to me that she and the boyfriend she was still living with had broken up.

As we walked out of the cherry orchard, I noticed that my cross necklace had fallen off. The sun was just beginning to rise. The woman noticed that I was feeling around my neck and into my clothes and asked what was wrong. I told her it was no big deal, but she insisted on going back to look for it. We found it in the spot we had laid down together all night. To this day I wonder if it was because it was my first time or if maybe I was drugged, but I can hardly remember any of the time we spent together in the orchard. I did have one more beer at the party that she brought to me before we ran off together, but I did not drink nearly enough to give me any sort of blackout.

I fell head over heels for this woman. I brought her gifts to work, and she brought me some. We slept together on one other occasion, but I was crushed within a few short weeks when I found out she had never broken up with her boyfriend. She was still living with him and she eventually told me the truth; this was more than I could handle. Not only was I now in trouble with the law again for violating my bond by drinking, I now had a completely crushed heart and different view of women. I always viewed women as being much more like angels than men. I knew that men lied to sleep with women, but I didn't think women would ever do such a thing.

And I had heard of men drugging women and then taking advantage of them, but I had never heard of a woman doing this sort of thing. Could she have possibly drugged me? Or did the guys who talked me into drinking drug me, and she just came along and took advantage of me. If I knew she had a boyfriend, I never would have entertained the thought of sleeping with her. This was all a lot to take in being that it was also the one-year anniversary of the car accident itself.

It is hard to know all the small details in life when dealing with people that are dishonest and selfish. The guy who threw the party couldn't tell me he was setting me up. Maybe the woman just felt sorry for all I had gone through and wanted to make me feel better. I couldn't help but feel like she was somehow assigned to me though. She had asked a lot of questions and was giving me a lot of unasked for counseling. What resulted from that night was, I received a broken heart and a new fear of being in trouble with the law. Sure enough, it wasn't long before I was contacted by my attorney who said I needed to come and see him because he got word that I got caught drinking.

Chapter 16
"Rehab"

I went in and met with my attorney who informed me that the prosecutor wanted to revoke my bond because he now knew I had violated my bond on two separate occasions. The prosecutor knew I had smoked marijuana when I lost my previous job, and he now knew I had drunk alcohol. I told my attorney that we should fight these accusations because the witnesses were a guy who smoked more marijuana than anyone I had ever met, and the other witness was a guy who probably drank much more then I had that night.

Besides, I didn't get caught drinking by chance, I got severely pressured into it; I was set up. My attorney said it was not wise to fight the prosecutor, that they had already discussed the issues at hand and that they both decided that if I would go to rehab that the offenses would be overlooked. My attorney advised me to go to rehab and told me it would only be a short outpatient program and then informed me that if I went to see my family doctor, I could get a referral from him and not have to pay much for the program.

I went to see my family doctor but thought that he would not give me a referral for rehab once he heard my side of the story. I didn't even want to drink at the party.

It was a simple case of me giving into peer pressure, not an addiction problem. I had not drunk any alcohol in a year. My family doctor didn't even care what I had to say. He said he believed I had a drinking and drug problem and that he would give me the referral that I needed. The only thing I could think of is that my attorney had already talked to my family doctor and told him I needed to go to rehab.

Rehab was different than I had expected. I imagined that it was going to be a lot like AA meetings, which the courts had initially made me attend. I had found that Rehab was pretty fun. I was meeting people that were forced to be sober from alcohol and drugs like I was, and we played fun games. I remember one game was a trust-building game we played where we would blindfold a person and have them trust us as we verbally guided them through a minefield of tennis balls and paper plates. These were part of our group meetings. I also liked hearing other people's sad stories. They made me feel like I wasn't the only one who was dealt a bad hand in life.

The part about rehab that I didn't like was when I had to meet with the counselor one on one. He continually tried to make me lie and confess that I was the driver of the car during the accident. I kept telling him that I was not the driver. This would upset him. He tried many ways to get me to confess, but I held my ground. He told me I was in a safe place and that anything I said to him would never leave the room. He asked me very personal questions. I didn't trust the guy because of the way he seemed to be trying different approaches to get me to say I was driving. I decided to do my own experiment with him one day. He asked me if I ever drank alcohol while I was on breathalyzers? I told him that I had a few times. A couple of days after telling him this, my attorney called me up and told me that the judge wanted to put me on two breathalyzers a day because he got word that I had drank while I was on them before. I told my attorney that I had never drank when I was taking them in the past, but that I had told my rehab counselor that I had, to test him and see if he was lying when he told me that anything I said to him was completely confidential and would never leave the room. Suddenly the judge no longer wanted me to take 2 breathalyzers a day.

When I met with my counselor again, I called him a liar and explained how I had lied to him to see if he was honest or not. This act really upset my counselor. He then took the gloves off and cut me down as much as he could. He told me that my problem was that I really was the driver but that I could not handle it mentally, so my brain was telling me I was not. That it was too much for my mind to take in that I was responsible for three kids' deaths. I told him that that was not the case. I had seen the other guy come from the driver's side of the vehicle to where I was. He was pulling hair out of his head saying he had to get out of there. I had seen another guy act like this on another occasion. I was in a different car accident a few years prior where the guy who was driving drove off a good size cliff and crashed into a cherry orchard. The driver got out of the car and fell to the ground and started pulling grass out of the field and kept repeating that he was in so much trouble. The guy in the back seat had a cut on his forehead that required 25 stitches. I had to yell at the guy on the ground to snap him out of his trance.

Besides seeing the guy pull hair out of his head while saying he wanted to run, I had also seen him come from the driver's side of the car. He crossed through the car's headlights and came to where I was standing off to the passenger's side of the vehicle.

Lastly, I read how this guy had changed his story to the police four times about who was driving the car. When someone keeps changing their story like that, it is obvious they are lying. I did not believe my brain was tricking me into thinking I was innocent because of what I had seen and heard. For this counselor to tell me I was the driver but couldn't handle the truth because of how painful it would be to me, I knew he was wrong. Besides, if it was a pain I couldn't handle, why did I remember the gruesome details of watching the one boy die right in my arms. And what the counselor didn't know, was that I also felt that their deaths were my fault. After all, I was the one who threw the party. It was also me who let the other guy drive.

I couldn't accept that some sort of pain of feeling responsible was stopping me from seeing the truth, because I felt the pain, I felt responsible. There was even a point that I was crying out to God to take my life and bring the other three back.

The counselor had not finished kicking me while I was down. Besides bringing back up all the emotions of feeling responsible, he started telling me that I was all alone. He said that everyone else in society knew that I was the driver of the vehicle. He also said that I had just told myself so many times that I was not the driver, that I began to believe the lie. That I had somehow tricked my own mind. He told me that everyone felt sorry for me because I couldn't see the truth. I told him that I was at the accident scene and I was not convinced because of what I saw. I told him no one else except me saw the guy come from the driver's side of the car while pulling hair out of his head while repeatedly saying he wanted to run. But my counselor was very persistent at telling me I was screwed up in my head and I needed serious help. He eventually broke me down, and I began to cry.

Was I really the only one who thought I was innocent of the crimes I was charged with? I felt guilty for the deaths of the three teenagers, but I was pretty sure I was innocent of the crimes I was charged with. What if the rest of society never sees the real truth and the courts convict me of something I did not do? What if they make me do

45 years in prison unjustly? All types of fears and dark thoughts were running through my head at this point. Suddenly my counselor switched completely around once he saw me crying. Now instead of telling me how bad of a thing this all was, he got excited and said it was a good thing. He started acting all crazy. He put two hands up like a wall in front of his face and kept peeking his eyes over them and then back below them. Each time he peeked over his hand wall he would say I can finally see you. The walls are coming down he said, as he took his hands down lower and lower. He said it was about time. He then tried one last time to get me to say I was the driver.

As soon as I told him I was not, he shot his hands back up and said there goes the wall; it is back up now. He then told me that if I didn't say I was the driver, he was kicking me out of the class. He asked if I wanted to stay in the class. I told him I did. The class made me feel good. He said all I had to do to stay in the class was say I was the driver. I asked him, wasn't the whole purpose of the class to address my drug and alcohol problem, that I still wasn't convinced I had. He told me that I was in too deep of a state of denial and that as long as I couldn't say I was the driver, we couldn't even address my alcohol and drug problem. He asked me why I even wanted to be in the class if I wasn't the driver? I told him I was having fun and was making some nice new friends. He told me that I was not there to make friends, to have fun and to play games, and then told me I was kicked out of the class. It now made sense that the entire reason the local authorities were trying to get me to violate my bond, was simply to get me into rehab where they could try and get me to confess to a crime I did not commit.

After a few days of being kicked out of rehab, my attorney called me up and said I had to appear in court because I quit going to my classes. I told him that I didn't quit, that I was told I couldn't go to them anymore. He told me it didn't matter if I quit or was kicked out, that I now had to go before the court to have a hearing on my bond violations. A friend of mine had told me that I just needed to jump through the court systems hoops and do whatever they say if I wanted to be left alone. But I wasn't going to lie and say I was the driver of the car when I was not. This was all becoming so frustrating and burdensome to me. I was starting to hate my life. Even though I felt I was at the end of my rope, there was still a small amount of hope. I remembered how relieved I felt when I had encountered God and gave my burdens to him on the day I had gotten saved. I went down to the beach by my house to try and get my mind off of what was happening to me, and that is when I experienced one of the greatest and most personal miracles ever!

Chapter 17
"Name in The Sky"

I lived around one mile away from my grandfather's beach. I walked down to his beach and sat in the sand by the water and began to tell God how hard my life was. I began to question if he could hear me; if he could see what I was going through. I was wondering if God saw what they were doing to me; how they charged me with three crimes I did not commit and were now trying to make me confess to them and how they had kicked me out of rehab because I wouldn't lie. While asking God all these types of questions, I looked up at the sky and saw a cloud in the shape of a "J". It looked like a capital "J" but didn't have the line of the top of it, like it was only the bottom portion of a capital "J".

It was a clear blue sky that day other than this one weird shaped cloud. I thought to myself, if that cloud had a top on it, it would look like a capital "J." Just then, a jet way up in the sky flew by and left a top on the "J." It was not a skywriting plane in case you were wondering. It was a jet that was way up high and for some reason only left a partial contrail. Now I was staring at a capital "J" just floating in the sky. I took this as a sign from God; a sign that he was telling me that he was listening to me and that he did see what I was going through. I bowed my head low, and with tears falling from my eyes, I began to tell him all about how my counselor kept trying to get me to confess to a crime I did not commit. I told him about how hard life was for me, about how I was scared to have to go to court for my bond hearing. I told him how bad I felt for three children that died and their families. I cast all of my burdens onto God at this point, and it felt great to do so!

To my amazement, when I looked back up, with tears still falling from my eyes, my entire name was written in the sky. It was all in capital letters. Capital "J," "A," "S," "H"! Most people get my name wrong and say or spell it with an "O" instead of an "A," but not God. I jumped up from the sand and ran home. When I got home, I excitedly told my parents all about what had happened. My parents' first response was very negative. They instantly thought I was either drunk or on drugs. Though they rarely used profanity, they had had enough! They thought I went out and violated my bond again by doing drugs and they started cursing and swearing up a storm. My parents were scared that they were going to lose their house because of me. But I quickly convinced them that I was not on anything. They asked how come I was shaking, talking really fast and acting crazy-like. I said it was because I just had another encounter with God!

My dad asked me who I thought I was for God to come off of his throne and come all the way down here to write my name in the sky. I wasn't sure how to respond to this. I didn't feel like I was any more special than anyone else. And how far away was God anyways? I had never really thought about it. I just told my dad that I did not know. My dad then asked if I thought I was special.

Suddenly my mother started crying hysterically. My dad and I asked her what was wrong. While pointing a finger at me, she yelled out in her tears, "You are retarded!" What? My dad and I both waited for her to elaborate on her accusation about me. I just encountered God again, saw a miracle, and she was calling me retarded because of it.

She went on to explain that it was from the car accident I was in. She said that I banged my head and now I am seeing things. I told her that the car accident was over a year ago, and asked why it would just now be affecting me over a year later. She thought for a moment and then said that it was because the brain injury was so deep in my head that it took over a year to wiggle its way to the surface. I told her that she was not a doctor and that that didn't make sense.

Both my parents were silent for a little while. They were still trying to figure out what was wrong with me, instead of rejoicing with me in the fact that God showed up in my time of dire need. My dad then asked if I had ever done any drugs that are known to give people hallucinations? I told him that I had. He excitedly announced that it was a flashback from the drugs I had done! But I had never seen anything like this while on the drug itself, why would the flashback be more intense than the actual times I was on the drug? I didn't truly believe that this was the best explanation for what I had just experienced, but my parents were relieved now. Suddenly my mother quit crying and said, "Oh good, you are not retarded. It was just from the drugs you have done in the past. They can't take my house away because of drugs you did before being on bond!"

I was glad that my parents were no longer attacking me and accusing me of being on drugs. I was also glad that they were no longer worried about losing their house, and were no longer calling me a retard. I had to be to work soon, so I left home and began walking to work. On my way to work, I started to tell God how sorry I was for doing drugs. I sarcastically asked God what I was going to see next because of the drugs. That is when I heard his voice as clear as day. He said, "It was not a flashback Jash." What? I quit walking and froze in place. I looked into the woods to see if he was standing somewhere nearby. The voice I heard was not with my ears, it was in the spirit, yet it was far more vivid than just a thought. I was very excited that he said my name. I was walking on the side of a paved road in the dirt and gravel shoulder portion when I heard God speak to me. I continued to look into the nearby woods, thinking that he might walk out of the woods holding his hand out as to shake mine and introduce himself to me. Then in my spirit, I asked him, "Who are you?" Just then, I felt a strong urge to look down on the ground. Laying right between my feet was a white plastic cross with Jesus on it. It looked like it came off of an inexpensive rosary. I quickly picked up the cross and stood there amazed while holding the necklace medallion in my hand. In my spirit, I now knew for sure that the voice I heard was Jesus Himself. I also knew He was the one who wrote my name in the sky.

With the cross in hand, I hurried to work. I was so amazed at what happened that day that I couldn't keep it to myself. I was a little fearful that if I told anyone, they might respond the same way my parents did, but now, besides just seeing my name written across the sky, I had also heard a voice, and I also had a plastic cross with Jesus on it in my pocket. I told one waitress I was working with that day about what happened, and within no time at all, I was called into the office by the manager. He told me that they accidentally overscheduled too many busboys that day and that someone had to go home. He asked if I wanted to go home. In my heart, I felt they just wanted the crazy religious guy who was hearing voices and seeing hallucinations to leave as soon as possible. But I didn't care. I couldn't wait to get home to tell my parents about what happened on my way to work.

When I got home I told my parents that it wasn't a flashback, that God spoke to me and told me that it was not, and that when I asked who he was, I found this cross right between my feet. Then I showed them the cross and asked them rhetorically if something like this could come from a flashback? My dad took the cross from my hand and looked at it in amazement and then quietly said, "Maybe you are blessed?" I am not sure how the cross got right between my feet as it did.

Usually, I see things on the side of the road while I am walking way before they are right between my feet. I often wonder if God just made it materialize right between my feet while I was asking him who he was or if he just blinded me to it until the right moment in time. No matter how or when it got there, it indeed was more than a coincidence that it was there right as I felt drawn to look down. It was either put there by God Himself or used by him.

Chapter 18
"Rain Prophesies"

I wound up quitting the restaurant job, but not before I had another job working at the Bower's Harbor boat marina by my house and right down the beach from my grandfather's beach. One day I went to work and told the guy I was working with that, "My friend Jesus says it is going to rain today at 2:00." I can't remember the exact time I told this guy, but the point is, it rained exactly at the time I told him it would.

The next day I went to work and told this same co-worker that my friend Jesus said it is going to rain at another specific time. To my amazement, it rained right on time again. I wasn't sure at the time why I kept saying it was my friend Jesus who told me this. It just seemed like I was picking a time and then saying this, but in reality, it truly was Jesus telling it to me and he was calling me friend.

I went to work and did the same thing two more days in a row. The times of the rain predictions were different each time. My co-worker did not like what was going on. I, on the other hand, loved it. It truly felt like Jesus was my friend. It felt like we were becoming best friends. On the fifth day, I didn't even feel like saying anything to my co-worker. But then I felt he was challenging me, more so, it felt like he was challenging Jesus. He looked across the harbor and could see a storm coming in. He then looked at his watch and then smugly said, "I say it is going to rain at 12:15". Then he stared at me like he was saying he could do it too. I looked him in his eyes and told him that, "My friend Jesus says a strong wind is going to come from the south and blow that storm north and that that the storm would return at 5:30 that evening!" I felt bad because there was an end of the year Labor Day party going on for the boaters at that time in the evening but then said, "oh well, that is what time Jesus says it is going to rain."

I got off of work early that day and returned to my home. I was very confident that I heard from Jesus at this point, so I told my parents that Jesus said it was going to rain at 5:30. They both laughed at me, but I knew they wouldn't be laughing once it began raining at the exact time I told them.

Later that day, when it was nearly 5:30, I looked out our living room window and saw that it was a clear blue sky. It hurt me to the core of my soul to see that the sky was so cloud free. My parents had a friend over at this time and told her what I had said about Jesus telling me it was going to rain at 5:30. Now, instead of just my parents, there were three people laughing at me. This made it hurt even more. It really appeared that it was not going to rain. I stepped out onto our back porch and began to ask Jesus why he would do this to me. He allowed me to predict the time it would rain four days in a row, and now he was going to let me look like a fool in front of my co-worker, my parents, and their friend.

As I was having this deep conversation with Jesus, he told me to put out my hand. So I stuck my hand out from under our roof's overhang. To my amazement, a drop of rain landed right in the center of my palm. Then there was another and another. I instantly had goosebumps shoot up both of my arms. I walked back into our house with a huge grin on my face and great joy in my heart. My parents looked at the clock and saw that it was exactly 5:30. They began to mock me and say, "didn't Jesus tell you it was going to start raining right now?" I looked at them with even a bigger smile on my face and told them that it was raining.

My parents and their friend looked out the window and saw nothing but blue sky, to them it still looked like a bright sunny day out. I forgot that the storm was going to come from the north and that our house faced south to make the most of the southern lighting. My parents were about to object and say it was not raining when my mom saw a few drops. She walked over to the window to investigate, and that is when the rain began to come down like a sheet of water. My parents were speechless. In my heart, Jesus, really was my friend, even though I didn't know how much of a friend he was to me yet.

The next day when I returned to work I was very excited and could not wait to tell my co-worker about how my parents didn't believe me, but then were speechless when it happened. To my disappointment, my co-worker was not there that day. Instead, my boss was there in his place. He told me that my co-worker thought I was crazy and requested not to work with me anymore. He then asked me about knowing when it would rain. Other people who I didn't know also began asking me if I knew when it would rain. I started getting paranoid because I didn't know these people and didn't have any word from Jesus telling me when it would rain. I told the strangers that I could turn on the land to sea weather station to see if it was supposed to rain, but they told me not to, and that they were just wondering if I knew when it was going to rain.

Somehow the topic of God's wrath came up, and my boss at the marina told me that God no longer punishes people, that he quit doing that in the Old Testament. In my heart, I thought my boss was wrong. Two days later, the boss's son came to work looking very upset. I asked him what the matter was. He told me that his dad woke up a couple of mornings prior with little red bumps all over his body. Then he explained how his dad made him sleep in his bed the next night to see if any red bumps would show up on him. I took this as a sign that God does punish people and that my boss was wrong. What bothered my boss's son the most, was not the fact that his dad used him as a human guinea pig, but he found out that his dad was a drug dealer that night.

Chapter 19
"Seeking God"

The time came that I had to go to court for violating my bond conditions. The court ordered that I begin retaking daily breathalyzers each morning like I was before. The court also ordered that I take a weekly drug test as well as attend Alcoholics Anonymous classes twice a week. I also had to either work full time or go to college full time. I was also still not allowed to drive any motorized vehicle.

My dad asked if I wanted him to buy me a horse to ride in and out of town since I wasn't allowed to drive. I couldn't see myself riding a horse into town, being that I had never seen anyone else do that in my town. I wasn't sure if it was legal or not. Instead, hitchhiking became my main form of getting around.

I decided to enroll in college full time. Up to this point, I was only going to school part-time. I took mostly art classes and was enrolled for a commercial art degree. The small community college I was going to had trimesters the first year that I attended. The year I decided to enroll full time is when they switched to just two semesters a year. That meant that all of the classes I had taken previously didn't count towards my degree.

I really liked taking art classes. I liked the people I was around, and I loved the way I could focus on the projects at hand and not think so much about the court system and the accident itself. The accident is something I could never get entirely off my mind. A person doesn't watch three teenage kids their age die and quickly forget about it. It is something I will never forget about. I began to seek God out more and more. Just as I could not forget the accident, I could not forget about how I had seen my name written in the sky either as well as my first encounter with God when I got saved. These were three major turning points in my life.

After seeing my name in the sky and seeing what Jesus could do, (as far as making it rain at a specific time each day and tell me about it beforehand), I began to seek God much more earnestly. I was amazed at how real God was and how present he is to us. I did not see him as an old grandpa sitting on a golden throne a million miles away from our planet who was unapproachable and unconcerned about us. I saw him as a close intimate friend. Seeing him as Jesus made me think of God as being younger and more active. Because of the way he kept showing up and communicating with me, I saw him as being intimate and concerned with our everyday affairs.

The more I sought out God, the more he showed up. At the same time, the more the devil began to show up as well. I didn't know how to seek God at first. I went to a church and a Bible study a few times, but they were very boring to me, and I didn't experience God there. I had a guy down the road from me who had started to tell me about the Native American ways. He was telling me about dream catchers and different events he went through. His three sons who were younger than me also began to say to me some very interesting stories. The youngest of the three said his dad could go invisible.

The children told me how they believed in spirits, trolls and shapeshifting (the ability to change from human form to an animal form). I found it strange that they really believed that a person could transform into an animal? I couldn't help but wonder, what if you can't change back, would you be stuck as a dog forever? Or what if you turned into a bird and your brain is so small that you forgot you were even a human, to begin with? I had many questions after hearing what they believed. I found it all very fascinating but was still very far from believing any of it.

I discovered that a couple of adult women that lived near my house believed in fairies. They even took me on a night walk through a forest that they said was enchanted to look for them. They genuinely seemed surprised when we didn't see any. They told me that they almost always see them. Then they had me do some sort of new age ritual to connect myself with the forces of the earth. They also believed in the power of crystals. They basically follow what is called a new age belief. When I tried to tell one of these women about God, she said to me that she believes God is a woman but that she is so humble that she lets everyone believe that she is a man. She also told me that her best friend was a spirit that has never had a human body but that it would channel through people to talk to her.

Chapter 20
"Indian Beliefs vs. Jesus"

The Indian beliefs guy gave me a book to read, and his son made me a dream catcher. He told me I had to find a feather to put in the center of the dream catcher for it to start working. I found a nice-looking feather and tied it to the center. After a few days, the child asked me if I had any strange dreams. I told him no. He came to my house and looked at my dream catcher and told me I had tied an owl feather to it. I didn't know what kind of feather it was that I had found in the woods. I thought it was a neat looking feather, and besides, he had never told me that it made a difference what type of feather I used.

The child then told me that an owl feather represents death and that I should not use one of them. He then told me he would get me an eagle's feather. I took the plastic cross that Jesus gave me when he told me that seeing my name in the sky was not a flashback, and tied it to the dream catcher. This made the child angry, and his voice dropped deeply as he told me I could not mix the two. I had no idea what he meant about mixing the two. At the time, I saw both beliefs as good. I thought that maybe you just couldn't mix the two good beliefs. Boy was I wrong?

The boy brought me an eagle feather from a bald eagle for my dream catcher. I was excited to see if the dream catcher was now going to work. The first vivid dream I had was of the sun setting really fast. Later that evening while my mother was driving me to an AA meeting we were driving towards the setting sun, and because there was a hill west of us, I saw the sun set very quickly as we drove towards it, just like I had seen in my dream. I sort of saw this as a coincidence, but couldn't help but think that the dream catcher may really be working.

The next night I had a dream of a square piece of the rainbow. I had never seen just a square piece of rainbow before and thought it a bit strange. I told a girl about the dream, and she said she was at a drum circle before and had seen one appear above the big drum that multiple people were banging on. Later that day as I was walking along the beach in my town I looked up to the sky and saw a square piece of the rainbow. Once I got home, I ran down to the guy's house who was teaching me about the Indian beliefs, and when I was about to tell him about the dream, I looked on his refrigerator and saw a new postcard he had gotten, that just happened to have a picture of a square piece of rainbow on it. I told him about the sun setting really fast as well as the dream about the square piece of rainbow. The guy told me to tell him about any future dreams I would have.

That night before I went to bed, I asked the dream catcher to give me another dream. I had a dream that night that scared me half to death. I dreamed of the devil. He was ugly looking, and his right horn was broken off. Seeing the devil isn't what scared me though. What scared me was that I felt like we were becoming friends. He had sort of an evil smirk on his face, and he was nodding his head up and down like he was saying yes to me. Later that day I saw a magazine on our living room floor. I flipped it over to its back and saw a music album's picture in an article, and low and behold; there was the picture of the devil with a broken horn on the band's music album. The title of the article was "Underground Music." It didn't seem coincidental that the word "underground" was in the article's title when the devil is often thought of as being in hell underground.

I went to the Indian beliefs guy's house and told him about my third dream. He himself wasn't an Indian; he just followed and taught their beliefs. When I told him about the dream, he got excited and said, "It has begun!" The freaky part about this was not so much what he said, but the way he said it. His voice lowered, and he now had a demonic growl to it when he spoke, not to mention he said this while rubbing his chin in excitement with a dark demonic looking smile on his face. He then told me that he had to get me into a purification lodge as soon as possible. He said he wanted to wait until the first snowfall, but that we had to hurry up now. I asked him what a purification lodge was, and he said it was like a sweat lodge and that he had to make one by hand. I imagined it was like a cross between a T-pee and a dry sauna. I was not looking forward to experiencing this. None of this was settling well with me.

I asked the pastor at the church I just recently started attending about the dream catcher, the dreams, and the purification lodge. He informed me that it was borderline witchcraft that I was getting into. He told me that when I was asking the dream catcher to give me a dream, it was like I was talking to an idol. He told me that we are not supposed to ask things made by human hands to do stuff for us like that.

Shortly after talking to the pastor, I began reading more of the book the Indian beliefs guy had given me. In the book, I kept reading about the "white man's war god" and the book called this god "Gesus." It didn't dawn on me at first that the one this book kept cutting down on was Jesus because it spelled his name "Gesus." If you pronounce the name Gesus with a "Gee" sound, it does sound like Jesus. I was surprised that I hadn't figured this out sooner. I was pronouncing it like one does "geese". But now my eyes were opened. I had taken mythology in high school and had just thought that Gesus was one of the many gods people use to believe in. But now it also made sense why one of his sons told me not to mix the two beliefs. Now I was terrified to continue learning about the Indian beliefs. I took everything this family had given me and returned it to them. I returned the dream catcher, the book and even a leather pouch they gave me full of tobacco that I was sprinkling onto dead animals to help them in the spirit realm. They were not home, so I just left it all on their porch.

I was then invited by the dad to come and talk at his house. I hesitantly accepted his invitation and took my dog with me. My dog was a very chill beagle. I had never once seen it mad at anyone or anything. The dad began the conversation by asking me why I returned everything? I told him about how I met Jesus and about how he wrote my name in the sky. I tried telling him about how Jesus was not a war god and the guy suddenly got very angry with me. He started to tell me that he was not about to let me be his teacher, and just then our dogs began to fight. For the first time I noticed that his dog had jet black toenails and it seemed like an evil spirit had taken it over. Our dogs had always gotten along before, but now they sounded like they were going to kill each other. He pointed toward his home's door and told me to leave. At which time I gladly ran out with my dog. A few other events I remember about this whole dark spiritual experience was:

1) A shape-shifting experience

2) An Alien Encounter

3) Book of trolls and

4) Invisibility.

But I will leave those stories for another day.

One of the most amazing things God showed to me, was that he controls the snow and the rain. But that is for another time and another book also.

Chapter 21 "Pentecostal Church/Getting Baptized."

Instead of following the Indian beliefs, I decided to declare that I was a follower of Jesus Christ publicly. The pastor of a small Pentecostal church had begun teaching on how important it was to be baptized. I started studying the Bible about baptism and decided it would be an excellent step to take, but not everyone agreed with this. In one of my college classes, I had two women in it that said they were witches and a third was often with them. The witch that appeared to be the leader of the three would sometimes come to class with them, but leave once class started.

The two witches in my class said that it was a bad idea to get baptized, and told me that I was making a big mistake. They tried as hard as they could to talk me out of going ahead with my decision. One day they told me the reason no one wanted to sit near me, was because I was a follower of Jesus. They said that was the reason why I didn't have any friends. Just as their words were taking root in my heart, two kids in the class came and sat by me; this made me feel better. I did feel quite friendless though. Most of my old friends were still partying away their lives. I couldn't drink or do drugs because I was on daily breathalyzers and weekly drug tests. Besides, I didn't have a driver's license, which made it hard to get to my friend's houses.

I went ahead with my decision to get baptized. This particular church usually did its baptizing in a nearby river, but it was late in the fall, and was way too cold for an outdoor baptism. They instead put a horse trough in their nursery room and filled it with water from a garden hose. There were probably around a half dozen other people that got baptized the same night I did. The pastor told me that I should try and speak in tongues after I came up out of the water. I heard other people that night speak in tongues for their first time immediately after they came up out of the water.

But I didn't experience it. However, I did feel a filling of the Spirit, and I felt like a fresh new baby. I was so filled with joy and did talk sort of like a drunken man. The water was very cold. I felt like I may have suffered a small case of hyperthermia. But even so, I felt very warm and tingly inside of me. It felt as though God himself was embracing me. I asked God to take away my cigarette smoking addiction when I got baptized, and after that night I was no longer a smoker.

When I returned to school and told the witches, that I went through with the baptism they again told me I made a mistake. There was a very dark spirited boy in one of my other classes that began telling me how I could do a ritual to renounce my baptism. He started to explain in detail how to perform the ritual, but I said to him I was not interested at all in renouncing it. Instead, I embraced it. To renounce my baptism would be to deny that I was a follower of Jesus. I had a few other run-ins with this bat boy that I won't go into detail about now. It is just very fitting that I call him bat boy.

A few days after being baptized, I was rudely awakened when my cat peed on my bed. The feline golden shower woke me up abruptly, and I had a vivid dream that faded away too quickly to remember it. I thought it strange that my cat did this because she never did anything like this before. I threw my bedding into the washing machine and took a shower and then headed to town for the day.

Later that day when I was in my class at college, I noticed only one witch was in class that day. She looked a little scared; she had her head hung low and would not look up at me. Then out of no where, poof, I suddenly remembered the dream I was having when my cat urinated on me. I was having a dream of this witch getting baptized. She looked up at me, our eyes connected, and then she burst into tears. She then quickly got up, ran out of the room, and never returned to class. I can only imagine what type of spiritual battle she was going through. Both of the witches dropped out of my class.

I never knew how real the spiritual realm was and how big of a battle was going on in it. While attending this Pentecostal church, the pastor would often refer to the devil. Which up until this point I could sort of see how the devil was in the picture. I figured it was the devil that tried to stop me from going to the church the day I got saved. It was also the devil that was working through the witches, bat boy, and other people who were trying to discourage me from following Christ. But up until this point, I didn't see the devil as the pastor was explaining him to be. He preached about how the devil is continually trying to attack us Christians.

The pastor told us that the devil is all around us every day, but the good news is, we don't have to be afraid because we have God's protection. I remember the preacher as describing the devil as a roaring lion but that this lion has had its' claws removed and its' teeth taken out. Then the preacher would start laughing out loud and talk about how he could feel the devil biting him right now as he was preaching. He said that it tickled to be gummed by the toothless lion and kneaded by its' clawless paws. The devil became far more of a reality once I began telling people on the street about Jesus.

Chapter 22 "The Devil at the Bar/Spiritual Warfare."

One day my friend and I were wondering what to do. My mother suggested that we go to a bar to listen to a couple of bands. We were not 21 years old yet, but it was college night at the bar, meaning you only had to be 18 years old to get in. I thought it sounded like fun, so I wanted to go. My friend, on the other hand, brought up the fact that we were now Christians, and we were not supposed to do that sort of thing anymore. I told him that it wasn't like we were going there to drink alcohol; we don't even smoke cigarettes any longer. I said we are just going to listen to some live bands play. Boy was I in for a surprise!

We got to the bar when there was hardly anyone there and picked out a table right near the front stage. The first band played, and it was a mellow hippie type of music. I enjoyed it but was hoping the next band would be better. As the next band was taking the stage and getting their instruments ready, three women walked over to us. I noticed that one of the women had an unopened pack of my old favorite brand of cigarettes in her hand. I asked her if I could have one. My friend looked at me shocked. I just smiled back at him. He then knew I was up to something. She said I could have one if I packed them for her. I packed those cigarettes like a pro and then opened the pack. I removed two cigarettes and asked if my friend could have one also. She said he could. By this time he had already figured out what I was going to do. We both put the cigarettes between our fingers and snapped them in half. The woman got very mad at what we did, grabbed her two friends, and walked away from us. I think they were waiting for us to invite them to sit with us. After all, we had a table that sat eight people, and it was just the two of us, and the bar was now pretty filled up.

As the next band was setting up, I noticed the drummer had a serious hunch back. He kept walking back and forth up to where the lead singer was setting up his microphone and then back to his drum set. I looked at my friend and made a joke about the drummer. Each time he walked up to ask the singer something, I would say, "Master, master!" and then say, "Yes Igor," as if the singer was responding to him.

The Holy Spirit instantly convicted me. I felt in my spirit that it was wrong to tease a man for his handicap, and the Spirit told me to pray for him. I started praying for the hunch backed man. I didn't stop there. I began to pray for everyone in the bar. Then to my surprise, the lead singer put a pair of costume devil horns on his head and then clipped a red pointed tail to the back of his pants which he ran up his back and over his shoulder. Making a grand entrance, the bass player came out dressed up as the grim reaper, and they began to play their music. You couldn't even see the face of the bass player. It looked like it could have actually been the real grim reaper himself.

The music they played was very hypnotic. This was when it began to get really strange. Most of the women in the bar came over to our table, and the band shifted sideways on stage so that they were now facing us instead of playing straightforward. The women started to rub up and down our bodies as the band started singing about coming to their world while telling us to choose one, just choose one. I looked over to where the men were all sitting on the other side of the bar, and one of the guy's eyes literally looked like they were glowing red, just like how you would see in a movie where they used some sort of special effects. But this was no filming trickery. I saw this as a manifestation of the devil himself. I was not afraid though. Instead, I was surprised how real he was. It was just like the pastor had said. The devil was always around us, but he couldn't hurt us because God was with us and the devil is like a declawed and defanged lion.

The lead singer was barefooted. One woman in the bar did not approve of what she was seeing, or she was an angel sent from God himself. The Bible says that God will make a way of escape. This women/angel took a lit cigarette and slammed it into the top center of the lead singer's foot. He screamed a horrific scream, and the women who were rubbing us looked like they fell out of the trance they were in. They were looking around confused like they didn't even know how they had gotten there or where they even were.

I looked at my friend and asked if he wanted to get out of there. He was more than ready to leave this bar. As we headed towards the door two of the bar's bouncers stepped in front of us to stop us from leaving. These guys crossed their arms in front of their chests. They had the biggest forearms I had ever seen. This is when I really leaned on the fact that the devil can't hurt us and I started walking towards these two guys. To my amazement, they both looked like they were forced against their will to turn towards each other, leaving left just enough room between them for us to pass through. Their entire bodies were shaking like they were trying to resist an invisible force. Just as I was about past these two behemoth men, I felt someone grab my coat. I thought one of them had grabbed me. I turned to look, and it was my friend. He was shaking like a scared little girl. He held onto my coat as we walked the rest of the length of the bar, which was well over 100 feet.

Once we got outside, my friend, let go of my jacket and began gasping for air. He had become paralyzed with fear to the point that he couldn't breathe when he was in the bar. I had only witnessed one other person this scared before in my life, and that was when he was face to face with death. While my friend was trying to catch his breath, an old friend of his came running out of the bar, grabbed him and told him to come back in. My friend pushed the guy off and yelled, "No!"

We began walking back to my friend's house, and it started to rain, so we took shelter under a church building's roof. He informed me that he had gone to a number of nightclubs in Texas that were cults. He told me we just witnessed a cult. He was very surprised that our little town had such a cult in it. This whole experience just all the more made me realize that there was an invisible spiritual war going on around us.

Chapter 23
"Hitchhiking"

When I was first released from jail on bond, I used to find rides into town and would usually bike the 12 or so miles back home. Most of my rides were with my dad and mom. As time went on, I began to look for other ways to get into town. I tried using our town's bus system, but I lived about ten miles out of town. Sometimes the bus would not show up, or it would take forever to get to where I needed to be because of the route the bus would take. One day I decided I would start hitchhiking. At first, I carried a small jackknife with me and would usually take a skateboard as well in case I didn't get picked up. I found hitchhiking was not that bad. I met a lot of interesting people that gave me rides. I lost my knife in one of the people's cars. I think I lost it in the guy's car that felt compelled to tell me horrible stories about hitchhiking. I don't know why the guy wanted to tell me such scary stories about something I found I had to start doing.

There were days when I had to hitchhike into and back out of town three to four times in one day. For example, if I had to take a breathalyzer first thing in the morning but then had a college class a few hours later and then had to take a drug test that evening, I would spend much of the day hitchhiking back and forth. Sometimes, I would just stay in town and find a place to take a nap, like on a park bench or in a classroom not being used instead of hitchhiking all the way back home only for a few hours. But this was always a little risky. One day I fell asleep in the grass at a park and ants began to crawl all over me and got into my clothes. Another day I fell asleep on a bench at the courthouse, and the judge who had thrown my parents in jail told someone to throw me outside because he thought I was a bum. On one occasion, while I was sleeping on a bench at the college I was attending, a girl decided she would see how many M&M candies she could put into my mouth before I woke up. On that occasion, I thought I was going to choke to death.

One of the most remarkable experiences I had while hitchhiking was when God proved to me that it was him giving me the rides. At the time, I was attending services at the small Pentecostal church. I was asked by a lady at this church how I was getting around. I told her that I was hitchhiking. She said God was blessing me with the rides. I told her it wasn't God. I believed that I would put out my thumb, people saw me, and out of the goodness of their hearts, they would stop and pick me up. I didn't see God as being involved at all.

The very next day after telling this woman that it was not God giving me the rides, I had to walk further than I had ever had to walk before while hitchhiking. I was almost to town before I decided to ask God if it really was him giving me the rides. The first vehicle to come down the road after I asked God this question, stopped. There were three, maybe four, Mexicans in the front seat of the pickup truck. They began to scoot over to let me up front with them, but I could not see four or five of us sitting in the front of a single bench seat of a pickup. They saw the look on my face and said I could jump in the back. At the time it was not illegal to ride in the back of a pickup truck bed. I jumped in the back and found myself in a whirlwind of dirt and rust when they got up to 55 miles an hour. I laughed and told God I deserved this for doubting it was him giving me rides. But it doesn't end there.

The next day when I first hit the highway, I told God I still wasn't sure it was him giving me the rides. I asked God that if it truly was him giving me the rides to please give me a ride before the church that was only a little ways down the road from my house. I had never been picked up that quickly, so I figured it would be a sign from God if I got a ride in that short of a distance. I saw a couple of cars coming, and they flew right by. Then as I was almost to the church, I saw one more car coming. I figured that this car was God 's last chance to prove to me it was him. The car flew by but then quickly slowed down and turned around in the church parking lot and then came back and picked me up.

I was amazed at this and told the guy who picked me up all about what was happening. He then told me that he was a pastor from a church a few miles past my house. I had lots of extra time to waste being that I got picked up so quickly, so the guy took me out for ice cream and told me all about how God must have a calling on my life since he is making himself so known in my life. He also said that he had a lot of similar things happen to him when God first called him into the ministry.

You would think this would be enough for me to fully believe that God was giving me rides each time I hitchhiked but I still had some doubts. God soon blew away every doubt I had when I hitchhiked home that night. I never started hitchhiking until I was on the highway that went to my house. Just before the highway was a church; I knelt down behind the church where they have a cross on their building and prayed. I told God I was sorry for still doubting but asked him to please prove it once and for all if it was him giving me the rides. I crossed the highway and saw the first car quickly approaching. It was a convertible, and it looked very fancy. The fancier cars rarely picked me up, and I had never been picked up by a convertible. I didn't even want to put out my thumb and give another rich man the satisfaction of passing me by.

But I heard the Spirit tell me to put out my thumb. I resisted at first, but the Spirit said it louder the second time. So I obeyed and put out my thumb just as the car was about to pass me by. To my surprise, the car slammed on its' brakes, and the driver yelled to me, "Get in!" I was so amazed by this, I had never ridden in a convertible before, and I was just as amazed to be picked up by the very first car. I had never been picked up this quickly while hitchhiking before. I told this guy the entire story, from the woman at the church all the way to kneeling down at the church by the highway. After explaining all of this to the guy, he said to me, "Guess what? I too am a pastor!" He then told me that he was from California and that the car he was driving only looked real fancy to me because I lived in a small town. He said that where he was from, his car was not very special. I praised God for proving to me that he was sovereign and that it was him giving me the rides.

After God proved to me that he provides, I no longer feared to have to hitchhike at all. Not only did he show to me that he provided the rides, he also proved to me that he protected me and fed me. One of the most amazing things God showed to me, was that he controls the snow and the rain. But that is for another time and another book.

Chapter 24
"Civil Case Attorney"

One day I got a call from my attorney, and he told me to come in and see him. Once at his office he said to me that my civil case was over, that they were concluding that I was the driver and we're going to settle out of court. I asked him why they had concluded I was the driver and he said he did not know and that he did not want to know either. He advised me that I should go talk to my civil case attorney about the matter. Her office was just a few blocks away from his, so I went there immediately.

My civil case attorney explained to me why they were concluding I was the driver. She said it was because they concluded that the driver of the car would have been more severely injured than the other surviving passenger. I told her that the other guy had more numerous and more severe injuries then I did; that if this was what they were basing their decision on, they were wrong. She said that I had to stay in the hospital longer than the other guy. I then informed her that the reason they kept me in the hospital longer was that they wanted to see if delayed chest injuries showed up on my chest and because they thought I had a memory loss from impacting my head. No injuries showed up on my chest, and I didn't have a memory loss from hitting my head, I had a memory loss because I was asleep while the other guy drove my car and crashed it.

Their conclusion did not make sense to me. She and I both knew the other guy had injuries to his head, shoulder, and neck. He was claiming that he could not work his job because of neck pains and headaches. At the same time, he was claiming the neck injuries and headaches; he was still singing as a lead singer in a heavy metal rock and roll band. He would scream into a microphone while standing in front of amplified speakers while headbanging. These are things a person could not do if they were claiming they couldn't wash dishes at a restaurant because of headaches and neck pains.

If anything, the singing gig is what was giving him the neck pains and headaches. The truth is, we knew he was lying about the headaches and neck pains, but the shoulder injury and the head injury he sustained were factual. He truly did sustain a good size bump to the head and an injury to his shoulder. Ironically, these two real injuries not only proved he sustained more injuries than I did, they also proved he was the driver.

My civil attorney told me it didn't really matter anyways, that my insurance company had to pay out money regardless as to who was driving. But I knew she was wrong. Maybe it is true that the insurance company had to pay out money to the families of the three deceased children, but it didn't have to pay the guy who was the actual driver and who was lying about half of his injuries. It really did matter, because if they concluded the opposite, and said they believed the real driver was the driver instead of me, that would have affected my future trial and probably got the charges dropped off of me instantly.

Chapter 25
"Appeal's Court Decision"

It took about a year and a half to get a decision from the State Appeal's Court. The judge had dropped the charges on me because he had ruled that the law I was charged with was unconstitutional. I never fully understood what the whole argument was about. What little I understood was that the law had a large punishment for a crime that was unintentional. The law was a fairly new law that I think somehow had its' roots from an organization called M.A.D.D. (Mothers Against Drunk Driving). From what I saw about this organization, it was a real hate-based organization that wanted blood. It reminds me of how the Old Testament in the Bible says, an eye for an eye. M.A.D.D. seemed to want people to be punished very severely if someone died regardless whether it was unintentional or not. I had heard that all three mothers of the children that died had joined M.A.D.D. I saw this organization as taking advantage of people who were already suffering a lot, just to push their political agenda. M.A.D.D. likes to demonize someone who may have just made one mistake in life, and then cry out for blood!

The scary thing about the law we were fighting, was that you could get zero years in prison or up to 15 years in prison. It didn't seem right that two people could unintentionally break a law and one could get locked up for 15 years and another not get locked up for even a single day. I can see how different factors can come into play. For example, if a person is completely drunk and runs over some people walking on a sidewalk or crosses a center line and hits an oncoming car, that person should get more time being they hit someone who had no say so in the matter. Verses two people out partying who get into a car by their own choice, fully aware that they both had a lot to drink, and they hit an electrical pole, and the passenger dies. In such a case, the deceased person did have a say so in the matter.

Or say a person already has had a couple of drunk driving crashes. In certain cases, I see the wisdom in having a range of how severely you can punish a person. I can also see how the court can easily abuse such a wide range of punishment.

From some other little understanding I had, about the whole issue of whether or not the law I was charged with should be considered constitutional or not, was the fact that no intention had to be proven, and, it didn't have to be proven that alcohol consumption was the main factor in the crash. We attended the Appeals Court Hearing, and I believe one of the arguments that was brought up was the fact that a person could crash from a deer running out in front of them and they would have crashed regardless if the driver had been drinking or not.

The Court of Appeals did not give a very long explanation for their decision. They basically just simply stated that our town's judge was wrong for ruling the law unconstitutional. I thought this meant that we would now go to trial, but my attorney told me that we were now appealing to the Supreme Court of the State of Michigan. The trial judge agreed to let me stay on bond while we appealed to the higher court level. I told my attorney I did not want to fight the law but rather wanted to go to trial. I told him I wanted him to prove my innocence. He said to me that it was not his job to prove my innocence, that it was the DA's job to prove me guilty, and his job was just to poke holes in the DA's case. My thought was, what better hole could he poke then to prove I was innocence.

My attorney then told me it was for the good that my trial was being pushed further into the future. He said people forget things as time goes on and that it will work in my favor. He also convinced me that fighting the law was a good thing because of all the other people this law would affect in the future. I felt selfish to not want to fight the law because of what my attorney said, but how come they would even argue this law over a crime I did not even commit. The real driver was not even over the drunk driving limit, so neither of us really broke this unintentional law. I remember wanting to fire my attorney one day because he seemed not to be doing what I asked him to do but instead seemed far more concerned about his own profit from this situation. Each time he saw his picture on the front page of the paper, he got excited. It was a good publicity for him. He wanted to run for a judge seat, and the more often he got on the front page of the paper the better it was for him. Besides this, he kept asking me if I wanted to try and make a plea-bargain with the DA. I told him I am not going to plea-bargain to a crime I did not commit. He then told me later that he talked to the DA about a plea-bargain, and the DA said no anyways. But then he would turn around and try to talk me into him going to the DA again and again with a plea-bargain.

I wanted so badly to fire my attorney one day that I began hitchhiking to town to tell him that he was fired, but no one would pick me up. I walked quite a long ways before it dawned on me that maybe God was causing me not to get picked up because he didn't want me to go through with firing my attorney. I was on top of a big hill and could see two bays from where I was. I then saw an eagle flying by. I told God that if he wanted me to turn around and return home and not fire my attorney, to have the eagle turn around and fly back the other way. To my amazement, the eagle did a hundred and eighty degree turn and flew back towards my house.

I didn't understand why God didn't want me to go fire my attorney, but I walked back home. As soon as I got home, I grabbed a Bible and asked God to tell me why I shouldn't fire my attorney? I opened the Bible, and the passage I first read was about Jesus telling his disciples not to pull up the weeds because they would also pull up the wheat. He told them that they needed to just let both the weeds and the wheat grow together until harvest time. I saw my attorney as a weed amongst the wheat. He wanted the publicity he was getting from my case but did not want to prove my innocence.

The trial judge of my case laughed at the Appeals Court's decision. He said it was only one page long and that his decision to rule the law unconstitutional was far more extensive and thus he was allowing me to stay on bond until we got a ruling from The Supreme Court. This meant I had to wait another year and a half before I would find out whether or not I had to stand trial for this charge or another charge. I was given a different attorney for the Supreme Court level. I was so excited about this. I couldn't wait to tell him about how I was innocent. My new attorney crushed my hopes when he told me he didn't care about whether I was innocent or not. He said his job was just to fight the law itself.

Chapter 26
"The Mob"

My life on bond continued, and so did my walk with God. I was very, angry at the guy who had thrown the party by my house, and pressured me into drinking, and then got me in trouble for it. He did this just to get himself off the hook but got me on the hook. I don't know why he was in trouble with the law to begin with, but I would guess it had to do with drunk driving because of how often he drank. I thought about getting even with the guy but read a verse in the Bible that says do not take your own revenge but rather leave room for God's vengeance, for vengeance is mine says the Lord. After reading that verse I let all my anger and any ideas I had of getting even with the guy go. It wasn't very long after that that the guy was out drinking and driving and crashed his truck into a tree and had to go to court for it. He had a real fancy truck that he greatly adored.

I saw this as God's way of paying him back for what he did to me. I don't like that people will get other people in trouble instead of just accepting their punishment for a crime they committed. I sat next to him when he had a court hearing one day, and he told me he was not going to get in trouble because he and the judge were really close. I told him that he was in trouble with me sitting right next to him. He suddenly began to shake in fear, especially when I saw an old friend of mine enter the courtroom in jail garb and handcuffs. I waved to my friend and pretended to take a picture with my fingers and then pointed to the guy I was sitting next to. My friend nodded his head up and down in agreement, and this made the guy next to me shake all the more. I felt bad for doing this and just lightly punched him in the leg, told him good luck, and then left the courtroom.

Seeing God take vengeance on this guy was just one of many times I have seen God repay people for the wrong they have done. Some would argue that it is not God but karma. Call it what you may, I now believe that God does avenge his children. Sometimes I witnessed God take instant vengeance on people in small ways, other times it was in much bigger ways. One time I had a friend laugh at me at work for spilling a little brick mortar out of a five-gallon bucket. I didn't find it funny and just left him in God's hands. Not even a half hour later he slipped off a board while pushing a whole wheelbarrow full of brick mortar and spilled the entire thing. I wanted to laugh but instead went and helped him get as much of it as we could back into the wheelbarrow.

While working at the marina, I began to worry about what they wanted to change the marina into. It was more or less a sailboat and yacht marina, and it was very peaceful. Then a cigar boat started coming around quite a bit. I had gotten word that they wanted to build a nightclub type of place there and serve alcohol. I believe this cigar boat kept coming from Chicago and I envisioned that once the nightclub was built, we were all of a sudden going to have a lot more of these cigar boats coming around. I pictured the place becoming a drop-off point for drug dealers from a bigger city. I did not like the attitude of the cigar boat owner for he was very rude.

I started looking more into what they had to do to make the place into a club and discovered that they had to convince our town hall into allowing this. I attended one of the town hall meetings and was surprised what was going on. The community was still mainly farmers and longtime residents of the area, but now our town's committee had been infiltrated by new people who were now our community's decision makers. I thought that maybe I could help influence our town into not allowing this place to be developed. The car accident I was in where the three kids died was only a mile away from the marina and on the same street as it. I figured just my presence would make people aware of the dangers of having a nightclub in the area.

I got word that Italians were somehow involved in the whole ordeal. This instantly made me think it was somehow tied to the mob. People started following me around, which made me paranoid. I ran from one of these people who were following me one day and ran to an old friend's house who lived near the marina. I wondered if it was the mob that was following me, then it dawned on me that my friend's family was Italian. I asked if they knew of any mob members in town. They said they did not, but they seemed a little nervous when I asked the question. They lived in a three-story mansion and were very well off financially. Another old friend was at this house and gave me a ride into town.

This friend was also an Italian. On the way into town, I told him I saw a car following us. He floored it down a few blocks to try and lose the car. He had a sport's car engine installed in his pickup truck and said he could lose the car. We flew much faster than I was comfortable with. He did indeed lose the car that was following us. But to our surprise, when we turned around another corner, there was a coast guard helicopter hovering over the road as if it too were looking for us.

After arriving at this guy's house, I asked his mother if she knew of any mob members that might be in town. She said she had heard of one named Tony, and then suggested I go downtown and hang out with friends. While hanging out with friends downtown I had an Italian guy come up to me and introduce himself as Tony. He said he heard I was looking for him. He then took me near the edge of the break wall and told me to look into the water. He said he had seen a garbage bag in the water earlier that day and it looked like it had a dead body in it. He said if it was a dead body no one would ever hear about it because our town doesn't make bad publicity like that known to the public. He was scaring me out of my socks. I didn't know how he may or may not be connected to the development of the marina by my house, all I knew is that he seemed to be trying everything he could to figure me out. He basically commanded a girl my age that I had seen around town a couple times to come over to him, and then asked what I thought about her. I felt she was somehow owned or controlled by him. I thought she was gorgeous, but I didn't know how to respond or what he was really asking me, so I just shrugged my shoulders.

Tony said he had just finished building a new hotel on the water and asked if I wanted to stay the night in one of the rooms. I said it would be nice, but instead of walking to the hotel, he took me to a hotel across the street from the new hotel; to a rundown old hotel. He showed me a room and said I could sleep there. Then he climbed into bed with me. He tried hugging me, but he discovered right away that I was not into this either. He wound up sleeping in a separate bed next to mine. He told me he had nightclubs in Chicago and asked if I wanted to be a bouncer at one. I said that would be cool, but that I was on bond and was not allowed to leave town.

The next day Tony took me to a secluded beach north of my town. He said it was a good place to swim. I swam for a little while and then returned to his car. He asked me if I had seen anybody in the woods. I told him I did not.

He said they looked like they were glowing white and he looked scared. I thought he was just being strange. He did have a picture of Jesus in the back seat of his car, a rosary hanging from his mirror, and his front license plate said "Jesus" on it, but I sensed he was not about the right thing, and I now believe God protected me that day with angels. For all I know, Tony was supposed to kill me that day. He drove an older model of a car that was light brownish in color. He said he and his friends all drove the same type and color of car.

One day while walking around the harbor by my house, I saw the same type and color of car that Tony drove about a mile away from me. I had a petrifying thought run through my mind saying that "the car's trunk would be slightly open, the back seat will be covered with plastic, and there is a sniper in the woods that is going to shoot me and then throw me into the trunk of the car." The fear was overwhelming. In hindsight, I am surprised I continued to walk towards the car instead of running home. I began to pray as hard as I could for God to protect me. As I approached the car, I noticed the back seat was covered with plastic and the truck was slightly open. I slammed the trunk closed and prayed even harder than I thought was possible. I began walking faster and looked into the woods to see if I could spot a sniper. I didn't see anyone, but I believed that there must have been someone out there because the thought was right about the other two-thirds of what went through my head; the trunk was open, and the rear seat was covered with plastic. Some people may say I am crazy and hearing voices in my head, but I believe God protects his people, and he wanted to show me just how real his protection was.

Needless to say, I left the whole marina fight up to the town hall and didn't pursue trying to interfere with the development of it. At one point a guy came into the marina dressed in overhauls and drove a pickup truck that looked like it belonged to a farmer. He asked how much he owed for the gas he put into his truck and then pulled out the biggest wad of hundred dollar bills I had ever seen. He flipped through them making sure I saw how much money he had. I got the impression he also worked for the mob because of the way his hair was slicked back and from all of the gold rings he had on his fingers. He certainly wasn't a poor farmer driving a beat up old truck.

A little while later I was at a store in town with my parents. I waited in the car while one of my parents ran into the store to buy something. In my spirit, I heard someone call my name. I looked around but didn't see anyone. Then I heard my name again. I turned completely around and saw two guys in a brand-new truck parked behind us. One of the guys was the guy who had the overhauls on who drove the old farm truck, but now he was wearing a fancy and expensive looking suit. They just stared at me. I felt like they were just testing to see if I would hear my name when they called it through their spirit. Or maybe the Holy Spirit called my name just to get me to see these guys. They did nothing but stare at me. It was pretty creepy I must say. Maybe they were supposed to shoot me but wouldn't do it while I was looking at them. I didn't take my eyes off of them until we drove away. God only knows who or what this guy and his friend were, and what they were up to. It was a demonic presence I felt both times I saw this fake farmer guy.

Chapter 27
"Barren Woman"

At this point in my life, I began digging deeper into the Bible. It took me a while to start reading it. At first, I found the Bible very boring. Each time I opened it to read, I would get really tired, even to the point that I would fall asleep.

One day while I was in college, I was trying to read it while sitting on a bench in the hallway. Just as I started to fall asleep, a woman came over and slapped her hand on my open Bible and greatly startled me because of how on the edge of sleeping I was. She then asked what I was reading. I told her I was in Matthew chapter One. She informed me that she had been observing me for a few days and told me that each time she saw me I was in Matthew Chapter 1. I told her about how I kept restarting at the beginning of the New Testament each day because I would fall asleep before I could finish the very first chapter. I was not much of a reader at this point in my life. I only read stuff that I had to. I had gone all through high school and had never read an entire book. I hated reading so much that I got mad if there was a back side to a one-page job application. She asked why I was trying to read the book of Matthew? I told her it was because I was told to start reading the Bible in the New Testament. She then started flipping my bible pages and told me to skip ahead to chapter 5 of Matthew. She said that it had a lot of red words in that chapter because that meant Jesus was talking himself. I didn't even know that most bibles had red words in them. There were no red words at the beginning of the Bible in the Old Testament where I had originally started to read.

I began to read the Bible from Matthew Chapter 5. I started to have all kinds of questions for this woman, especially once I got to the portion of Matthew 5 that talks about adultery. I asked her if it was wrong for me to have slept with a woman that I wasn't married to? She instantly took offense and told me at least she was not pregnant. What? Wait a minute! Hold up there! What was she talking about? I asked her about me, not her. It was obvious to me that she was sleeping with a guy and felt guilty about it. It rubbed her the wrong way when I asked her this question. Shortly after that day, I didn't see her around anymore. I asked another college student what had happened to her and they informed me that she had dropped out of school because she was pregnant. They also told me that it was extremely hard for her family because they were so religious. She was either pregnant at the time she blurted out to me what she did, or became so shortly thereafter.

My friend's grandmother was also one of the first people to help me start reading the bible. She was one of the first people I knew that could quote scriptures from memory. She also had some fascinating stories about how God was active in her life. She told me about how her eyeglasses fell off her face and into the water at the end of her dock. She said she cried out to Jesus to help her because she could not go into the water to get them. Then the Lord spoke to her and told her to follow a fishing bobber that floated by. The bobber floated up to the shore and underneath an overturned rowboat that was part way in the water. The Lord then told her that her glasses were under the boat. She shoved the boat over a little, and there were her glasses!

Wow! I was amazed by her story. I had stories of my own, but to physically move her glasses amazed me. To this day I wonder how God moved her glasses? I do believe God can do anything. He could have just teleported her glasses to the shore, but I think he had a bobber float by with a little bit of fishing line and a hook attached to it, snagged the glasses and dragged them to shore. It reminds me of the time in the Bible where Jesus told his disciples to go and catch a fish and that they would find a coin in its mouth to pay the temple tax with.

I am not sure why God does things the way he does, but I stand amazed at what he does. He uses everyday things around us to bless us. Just a few weeks ago I needed a washer to fix my license plate that the bolt broke through. I looked down at the ground, and there was the perfect size washer that I needed not even two feet away.

That is when I looked up and begin to thank the Lord. Some people say things like that are just a coincidence, but I believe they are blessings from God. On many occasions, I have spent much time getting just a single washer. You first have to drive to a hardware store, then locate the washer department. Then you must figure out the size and kind you need. Then when you add on the time it takes to drive home, you can spend a few hours just getting one small round piece of round metal. But not the other day. I felt that drawing of my eyes to a grassy spot a few inches off the driveway I was in, and bingo!, there was exactly what I needed.

Some of the things seem so trivial in the overall picture, but God is a loving Father in heaven concerned with even small matters in our lives. He often smooths out even small irritants in our lives. The opposite is true for those who don't love God and resist His Spirit. The small day to day matters is the opposite of blessings and more along the lines of curses, small irritants are magnified into large ones.

I became extremely fascinated with the Bible once it started to come alive in my life. Sometimes certain verses would jump off the page at me and penetrate my heart profoundly. One time this happened was when I was reading the book of Luke. In Chapter 1, verse 36, the Bible talks about this woman who was now six months with child. It says this woman was called barren. I started thinking as hard as I could about where I had heard this word "barren" before. Then it dawned on me that the women who took my virginity told me she was barren. That was the first time I had ever heard this word before. I started doing the math and found out that it was exactly six months to the day that I had slept with her. Suddenly, I believed God was telling me she was pregnant. I asked how it was possible? I looked back at the Bible, and the very next verse said that with God, nothing shall be impossible.

As much as I never wanted to see this woman again, I had to know if she was pregnant. I went to her house and hid in her bushes. Not long after hiding, I saw her pull into her driveway. I looked as hard as I could at her stomach wondering if she looked pregnant, but I didn't even know how much a six-month pregnant women would be showing, besides, it was cold out, and she had a heavy jacket on. I stepped out of the bushes, and just about gave her a heart attack. I asked her if she was pregnant? With almost a tear in her eye, she told me she could not get pregnant. I wondered if maybe she lied to me. She had lied about not being broke up with her boyfriend after all. I told her about how I went to a church and laid on the steps and asked God to make her able to have kids. I was too scared to go inside the church that night, and just prayed for her while on the outdoor steps. I also told her about how I read in the Bible about how a woman who was said to be barren was now sixth months pregnant, and that it was exactly six months to the day that we made love.

She told me not to take the Bible so serious. How could I not though? The Bible kept coming more and more alive in my life. I then considered the entire experience as God letting me know that he heard me when I prayed on the steps of that church. He just did not answer the prayer the way I had hoped he would. As the saying goes, thank God for unanswered prayers. I figured that this woman would not have been a good wife to me or a good mother to my children. She was not a faithful or honest woman.

Chapter 28
"A Drunk Angel?"

As time went on, I became extremely spiritually hungry. I started going to any Bible study I could find. I went to any and every church I was invited to or felt lead to go to. One place I really enjoyed going to, was a high school youth group. I was in college, but I didn't know of any college-age youth groups that I could attend. The youth pastor didn't mind me attending the younger aged youth group. He was no ordinary youth pastor. He was really driving the word of God home into the hearts of the children. I couldn't get enough of this youth group. I started to borrow praise and worship music tapes from this youth group to listen to during the week. I had a Walkman tape player that I took with me everywhere.

I began to tell people on the street about Jesus. I wanted everyone to have what I had. I had never felt so good in my life before. Even though I was going through a hard time in my life, I still had an indescribable peace and joy. It was hard having to hitchhike in and out of town and walk everywhere. It was also hard to attend AA meetings and be persecuted for believing in Jesus. At one of the meetings, I was pulled aside at the end of the meeting and told to not tell people who my higher power was. One woman at AA had just had her sister die. I listened to people try and comfort her and talk about how alcohol kills, but I told everyone she just needed a hug. I got up and hugged her and gave her the plastic cross I had in my pocket that Jesus had given me on the side of the road the day he wrote my name in the sky. I told her that the cross was blessed. The hug and the cross lightened her spirit and heart far more than people telling her about the negative effects of alcohol, and she thanked me for them both.

Life was also hard because I wasn't used to having only a few friends. It also was a burden to have to get to town early every morning, 366 days in a leap year, in order to take a breathalyzer. It was also extremely heavy to my heart to think that I might be spending 45 years in prison for a crime I did not commit. In spite of all the difficulties I had, having Jesus in my life made it bearable. Singing praises and listening to praise music gave me joy. One day while I was walking downtown to go and tell people about Jesus, my batteries died in my Walkman. I looked up to heaven and asked God to help me get new batteries because I didn't have any money to purchase any. I then told God that my headphones were not working very well either. I was a poor college student and was hoping that God would somehow supply my need.

I got downtown and saw a group of kids a little younger than myself and went over to talk to them about Jesus. They asked why I was telling them about Jesus? They said I should go tell the drunk guy on the beach about Jesus instead. I told them they needed Jesus just as much as he did, but I decided to go and talk to the drunk guy. They couldn't believe I was going to go talk to him and they followed close behind me and listened for a little while.

The drunk guy was very unaccepting of what I had to say at first. The kids soon walked away. I am not sure if he just wanted to act tough around the crowd or what, but before I knew it, he did a 180-degree turn. He suddenly got excited about what I was saying. It seemed like he saw something on the distant hillside that made him change his demeanor. I looked to see what he may have seen and all I saw was a telephone pole on the hill that looked like a cross. Maybe he saw this and thought it was a cross, and/or a sign. Whatever it was, something made him change. He got excited, thanked me, and wanted to give me something to show his gratitude.

He first offered me the few beers he had left. I told him I didn't drink. He then looked around to see what else he had, and he grabbed his dual tape deck radio and shoved it into my chest. He told me to take the radio as he pressed it into me. As I took the radio from him, I felt a spiritual shock blast through my entire body. It was as if God himself handed me the radio. It even had brand new batteries in it. I went to thank the guy, but he had already walked off at a brisk pace. I followed after him but couldn't catch up to him. He walked around a building, and I quickly walked around it a few seconds after him, but he had disappeared. I looked up and down the alley for him. I didn't see any place he could have ran to and hid. I wondered if he was an angel or not. I can't say he was drunk for sure. I do know he had a beer in his hand and other beers with him, but I didn't ever see him drink one. I concluded he must be an angel because of how he vanished into thin air. The bible says that we sometimes entertain angels unaware. Maybe the beer was just a test. If I had taken the beer, I never would have gotten the better treasure, which was the radio and the awesome feeling I received when he handed it to me. And who is to say angels cannot drink anyways.

I no longer needed new batteries, my headphones, or Walkman because I had a radio now that had two speakers attached to it. I took that radio, just about everywhere with me. One day I got tired of listening to the tape player, and I turned on the tuner part of the radio to listen to the local radio stations. I didn't like any of the secular (normal) music anymore after discovering music that would pump up and feed my spirit. I said to God that he needed a radio station that played Christian music. I didn't know what station to listen to. I felt lead by the Spirit to spin the tuner dial three quick turns to the left and to listen to the station it landed on. The song that was playing on the station the tuner had landed on, was a song I had never heard before. After a minute or so I realized that it was a

Christian song. I was blown away! I thought God made me a Christian station on the spot. Later I discovered that the station had already existed, I had just never heard of it before. It was 89.9 WLJN. WLJN now has a sister station that I love to listen to called 95.9 FUEL. The radio truly was a blessing from God. The batteries never died, and God used it greatly in my life.

Chapter 29
"My Brother's Car"

I began preaching more and more on the streets. I would go to the mall, to our downtown, to a local ski resort, a bowling alley, anywhere and everywhere that there were kids who needed to hear about Jesus. I talked to adults as well, but most adults seemed so closed off to listening to me when I was a still a teenager myself. The kids, on the other hand, were hungry for the truth that the society was hiding from them. Some of the kids though would laugh at me. Pretty much every kid would laugh at me at first, but most of them would change their demeanor after thinking a little bit about what I was saying. Some of the things I would say would be from the Holy Spirit himself. I remember one kid telling me he was good and didn't see a need for being saved. I told him it was wrong to steal from his sister. His mouth dropped open, and I could tell he began seeing his need and also began repenting in his heart. I didn't know this kid at all. Neither did I know he had a sister, much less that he stole from her. Whenever this would happen, it reminded me of when I first got saved. How the pastor said things that no one else could know about me.

My brother had a number of friends that were laughing at me behind my back. My brother said I needed to stop telling people about Jesus. I told him God wanted me to keep telling people about Jesus. My brother got mad and told me people are laughing at me. People almost always laugh at me. I do and say strange things. I actually try to make people laugh. But I would much rather people laugh at me for doing something good, something God wants me to do, then how people laughed at me when I would get drunk or do drugs. I would do stupid stuff when I was not sober. Stuff to make people laugh.

I understood that my brother was actually concerned about me, but I couldn't stop doing what God was telling me to do. My brother persisted in telling me I needed to stop. I got frustrated and yelled out, "Your car will no longer be with you in two weeks!" I didn't know why I said this. I'm not sure if God put it on my heart and it was going to happen whether or not I told him, or if I cursed his car and caused it to happen. None-the-less, two weeks to the day my brother still had his car. I had forgotten about even saying what I did, but my brother had not. He was all smiles when the two weeks were up and he still had his car. When he went to leave work that day and tried to start his car, something fell completely out of it and onto the ground. I think it was his transmission.

He called our mother on our work's phone and after a few minutes handed the phone to me and told me she wanted to talk to me. She asked me what I did to his car? I told her that I had not done anything to it. She then asked if I told him his car would no longer be with him in two weeks? Then I remembered what I had said. It was two weeks exactly to the day. It was probably even to the exact minute. In any case, after this incident, my brother never told me to stop preaching again and he now goes to church regularly. My brother was a teenager at the time like myself. A car means a lot to a person when they are a teenager.

Chapter 30
"My Dad Sees the Light"

My dad was a little concerned about me reading the bible as often as I was. At one point he said to me that only the priests were supposed to read the bible. I told him there is such good stuff in the bible and that anyone can read it. My dad started listening to WLJN the Christian radio station. He was working the night shift at a factory at the time.

On his way home one extremely hot night, the preacher on the radio started preaching about how if your life is not right with God your soul knows it. The preacher preached about how you will feel the flames of hell inside of you. Then the preacher asked those listening to the radio if they could feel the flames inside of them, if they were hot, if they could feel the heat.

My dad started talking back to the preacher on the radio. He told the preacher that he could feel the heat, that he was hot. My dad could feel the heat both spiritually and physically. His new pre-owned car that he had recently bought only had one window that worked. The driver's side window would roll down, but the passenger's side window would not. He had taken the passenger's side door apart and tried everything he could think of to try and get the window to work. He said that the previous owner must have known about the window not working because there was a piece of wood that was holding the window up. Due to the fact that only one window in the car would roll down, my dad could not get a cross breeze going in the car to cool off.

The radio preacher then said to call on Jesus; that Jesus could cool the flames and save them. The preacher said that Jesus can help you! My dad called on Jesus and asked him to help him. He called out and asked Jesus to please roll down the other window in his car as he pushed down on the passenger's window button. For the first time since he had owned this new car, the passenger's side window went down.

When my dad told me this story, I was very excited. Part of me wanted to ask my dad if he had ever done hallucinogenic drugs, and then suggest that maybe it was just a flashback like he had done to me when I saw God write my name in the sky. But I didn't want to dampen the excitement of my dad encountering Jesus. My dad seemed much happier in life after this experience. I think Jesus did more than cool my dad down physically that day. I think he also cooled the flames of hell in his soul.

After this, my dad got himself a Bible and started reading it for himself. I was glad that my dad was no longer trying to explain away the miracles I was experiencing and was starting to experience them himself.

Chapter 31
"Evangelism Class"

I loved telling people on the street about Jesus and seeing how they would respond to it. When I had started attending a new church, I found out they had an evangelizing class where a number of people would meet up and learn how to evangelize, and then hit the streets and put what they learned into practice. I felt like I had already had a lot of practice doing this type of thing, but found the class a little helpful. The main problem I had with the way they did things though, was how mechanical they tried to make evangelizing. We had certain scriptures we had to memorize, and a certain procedure we were to follow when talking to people. We were also supposed to put together a certain length of a testimony we could share with people about what difference Jesus has made in our life.

I remember going out with the few people in our group and trying to do it the way I was instructed. It didn't seem all that effective or genuine. The main guy we talked to was verbally aggressive to us. I likened him as onto a pit bull. But when I went off script and just let the Spirit speak, his aggression melted away. It was like the pit bull turned into a poodle. He was eating out of the palm of our hand after that. I can't recall what I said to him, but I knew that evangelism couldn't always be done in a certain set format. Don't get me wrong, you can learn some good stuff from such a class, but it is not necessary. The main thing is to let God have control and to say what he wants them to hear. Just make yourself available and ask God to use you. Jesus reached to people in a number of different ways when he was on earth, and he is still using many different ways to reach people today. Sometimes he told people things only he could know about them. Other times he healed them or raised them from the dead. One man, he freed from a bunch of demons which caused him to accept Jesus. Another strange incident is when Jesus used his spit to give a blind man sight.

Chapter 32
"Interview with a News Reporter"

My local newspaper contacted me one day and said they wanted to run an article on me. The reporter who contacted me wrote for the religious section of the paper. I met with her and told her all about getting saved and about how Jesus wrote my name in the sky. She was amazed.

A few days after our interview, she sent a photographer to the evangelism class I was in to take a few shots of me. At the time, she seemed very excited to write the article about me, but then she called me up and told me she wanted to meet with me a second time. I met her at the mall and right away I could tell that she was not happy. She said to me that her boss told her that their newspaper was not a tabloid paper and that they were not going to print an article that was not true.

She said she believed everything I had said to her. The funny thing was, the paper was constantly writing articles about me that were untrue. I believe that there were over one hundred articles written about the accident and court-related things dealing with it. Both my trial attorney and my civil attorney had requested that my cases be moved out of town because of the fact that any potential jury members were already told too many times the lie that I was the driver of the car. The paper would print the lies about me, but they refused to print a true event that happened in my life. The news reporter told me she was sorry. I told her that it was ok. It hurt inside to see this media outlet so willing to spread lies about me, but not willing to speak the truth.

It was not just the local newspaper. The two main television news stations also slandered me countless of times on television over the nearly four years I was on bond. I was tried in the media way before I ever stepped foot in the courtroom. The media most certainly does not follow the philosophy that a person is innocent until proved guilty. They just yell out to anyone who is willing to listen their big fat lies. It is no wonder they are now being labeled as "The Fake News Media." I don't believe all reporters or media outlets are this way, but it seems that many of them have chosen to go down this path of darkness.

The reporter later contacted me and told me that she had quit working for the newspaper and had become fully involved in mission work. She was excited to tell me that God had also repeatedly done things in her life that were amazing. It is always a beautiful thing when someone else has God begin to show up in their lives in a real personal way. God wants everyone to be saved and to have a personal relationship with Him, but before people can even really accept the gift of eternal life, or begin this kind of relationship, they have to be made aware of their need for it, they need to be aware of their need for Jesus. Then they need to humble themselves and truly accept Jesus Christ as their Lord and Savior.

Chapter 33
"A Homeless Man Sees the Light"

One day when I went to go to a new youth group I had never been to. I got the time wrong and showed up an hour early to the church that it was at. I didn't know what to do with the extra time I had, but then I saw some homeless people at a nearby park. I walked over to them and began talking to them about their need to be saved. A couple of them laughed at me, but one of the guys looked like he was about to cry. He told me about how alcohol was wrecking his life. He said he just couldn't stop drinking. He informed me about how he had a new job that he was supposed to go to that day but instead chose to get drunk.

The homeless man then told me he wanted a new life. He was suddenly aware of his need for Jesus. I took him away from his drunk homeless friends who were being very sarcastically rude and disruptive, and I told him to repeat a prayer with me.

I looked up to the heaven and said "Jesus" then waited for him to say it. He looked up and said "Jesus." At that very moment, a sunbeam burst through the clouds right onto him, and he immediately fell to his knees. He looked up at me from his kneeling position, and I held my hand out for him to grab. He looked as though he had seen an angel or a ghost, or an angel ghost. His eyes were now open as big as possible, and he was trembling. He looked as though he was trying to speak, but was unable to do so. He reached out, took my hand, and I helped him to his feet. We slowly walked back to the picnic table and sat down. I was waiting intently to hear what he had to say. I knew he had experienced something miraculous, something supernatural. I was going to lead him into a much longer prayer than just one word, but it was obvious that that was all he needed.

After waiting a few minutes and seeing this guy sit there still lost in amazement, I saw him getting ready to say something. I was expecting him to say something profound. As his mouth began to slowly open, I leaned in closer to listen to him. To my surprise, out of his mouth burst puke! Thank God none of it got on me. I just left him there that day and went on to attend the youth group. I wondered though if he saw Jesus in the sky. I know in my heart that he saw the light that day, spiritually speaking, but I still wonder if with his physical eyes he saw me as Jesus when I offered him my hand to help him up. After all, Christ lives within us. He lives within all of his followers.

Chapter 34
"Supreme Court Decision"

It took around another year and a half for the Supreme Court to make a decision. They sided with the Appeals court and declared that the law was constitutional. They basically said it did not matter if alcohol was a factor in the crash or not, that a person should still be held accountable. They went as far as to say that even if a motorcycle crosses the center lane and hits an oncoming car, that if the person driving the car is over the limit, they are the one who is responsible because they should not even have been on the road.

They basically declared that even if the motorcyclist is completely at fault for the crash, blame should still be put on the one who was drinking. This seemed wrong to me and still does, but I didn't ever really care all that much about the constitutionality of the law. I was far more concerned about the fact that I was not even the driver of the car. It seemed strange that they were now basing their drunk driving laws on a crime that never even happened. Yes, three people did die, but the real driver of the car was not legally drunk.

By the time they took a blood sample from me at the hospital, I was not over the drunk driving limit either. They then got a warrant and confiscated the blood that was taken from me for medical tests and tested it for alcohol content. It was at .102 percent, which was 2 one-hundredths over the drunk driving limit. That means I was one small sip over the limit. Then they were arguing whether or not the alcohol level in my blood had risen after the accident and maybe peaked out right as they took the blood for medical tests and that I may have been under the legal limit at the time of the accident. I don't know why they even needed blood for medical testing. I had no major bleeding or anything. The only injury I sustained from the accident was one small bump on the right side of my head. I don't think they really needed blood for medical testing purposes, but rather that was a sly way they could get blood to later use to test for an alcohol level. It was probably just an unethical way to preserve blood until they could get a warrant.

At this point in my life, it had been over three and a half years since the accident, and they were about to take me to trial.

My original trial attorney had gotten so much publicity from my situation, that when he had run for a judge seat, he won and got elected. I was then given a new trial attorney and told I had to stand trial. This was at least the forth attorney I had to represent me. Two trial attorneys, one appellate attorney, and one civil case attorney. I was excited to have a new trial attorney and couldn't wait to tell him about my innocence. When I told him I wanted to prove my innocence, he told me word for word what my last trial attorney had told me; about how it was not his job to prove my innocence but rather the DA's job to prove me guilty, that his job was just to poke holes in the DA's case. What? Do they teach this stupid philosophy to all the attorneys at law school or did my last attorney tell him what to say if I brought up the subject of my innocence?

I felt like I was living in a nightmare. I couldn't believe how unconcerned everyone was about the truth, and for justice. It wasn't right that the guy who crashed my car was awarded thirty-six thousand dollars by the insurance company. It was as if he was being paid for killing three children and to lie about it. It was also not fair that they charged me for the deaths and were making my life so miserable. If it was not for Jesus in my life, I think I would have lost it a long time before this period of time in my life and probably have hurt myself or others.

AA got to the point that I could not stand the amount of persecution I was getting there. So I wrote the judge a letter and hand delivered it to his desk asking to attend Bible studies instead of going to AA. He said I went about asking him wrong, that I was supposed to go through an attorney, but then granted my request. I couldn't stand any of the attorneys I had. This latest attorney reminded me of Simba's evil uncle Scar in the Lion King movie. He had asked me if I wanted to fire him, and boy did I ever want to, but I now had a trial date, and I didn't know how to represent myself and felt I did not have time to figure it out.

My parents and I attended the oral arguments at the Supreme court level. I don't recall much of what was said. I just remember that some of the reasoning behind the law seemed ridiculous. At one point, someone said drunk driving was as dangerous as shooting a loaded gun into a crowd of people, that a person knows they are going to hurt someone if they drive drunk. I didn't know how they could reach such a conclusion. If you shoot a gun into a crowd of people, someone is most certainly going to get hurt and probably die. I had heard of, and personally seen, thousands of occasions where people drove drunk and didn't hurt a single person. It seems that 99 percent of the time, if not more, people drive drunk and don't hurt anyone.

The opposite is true if you shoot a gun into a crowd of people. If you shoot a gun into a crowd of people, you will probably hurt or kill someone 99 percent of the time. I don't endorse drunk driving, I just think they have gone too extreme with their logic against it. My town probably has forty bars in it, and every night thousands of people drive after drinking, but it is rare that you hear about someone dying because of it. Don't get me wrong I do know that drunk driving can be dangerous, more so for some individuals. I knew some guys that I called lightweights that could not even drink a couple of beers and drive. After one or two beers these guys were driving down sidewalks. Alcohol certainly seems to affect some people more severely than others. I believe cell phones cause people to be worse drivers then alcohol. But that subject opens a whole new can of worms.

Chapter 35
"College Youth Group"

The Bible study/youth group I enjoyed the most later on in my spiritual walk was a college-aged one that was run by college-aged students. Many of the young adults that attended this group were dedicated to serving God. It was nice to see people my age who were seeking to follow Christ. They all seemed so pure to me. Many of these young adults had never even seen drugs much less tried them. I doubt many of them had even ever drank alcohol. I was so impressed with their love for God and their obedience to him. I would say the majority of these college students were still virgins as well. I felt unworthy at times to be a part of their group.

One day they all laid hands on me and prayed for me, and I broke out into tears. While they were praying, I could sense Jesus right there in front of me. I couldn't look at him, but rather bowed my head and told him he could let me go. I said this because I felt he had plenty of enough good young adults following him, and that I couldn't be as good as them. He told me he would never let me go, which made me cry even harder.

I started attending this college group meetings when there were around ten people going to it. I almost quit going right away, but there was a cute girl there that caught my eye. Before the end of that summer, there were around 100 college aged kids attending it, and it was mostly cute girls. Girls that radiated with the glow of heaven. One of the guys continued it through the school session months at our small community college that I was going to, but most of the kids that attended the summer group left our town to go to bigger colleges and universities in bigger cities.

The following summer there was even more young adults attending the group. It was an awesome experience to be surrounded by so many people my age wanting to be closer and closer to Jesus. The group was well structured. When you walked through the door, I remember they would hand you a piece of paper that had a short message on it that lined up with what they would be talking about that night.

They would tell you to go and find a quiet place in the church to read the message. At the end of the message, you were to pray about the subject and reflect on how it affects or applies to your life. The praise band would then start playing a song, and you were to come into the main room whenever you felt you were ready. By the end of the night, you were very spiritually impacted by what was sung and said. Not every week was structured the same way. Sometimes they started with an icebreaker and then went into singing. Other times they would give a short message to start with and then sing. I remember also splitting into small groups at times, so we could each share the knowledge we were receiving from God and to more personally get to know God and each other.

I really loved how they often had songs that pertained to the message that day. I always think it is good when a praise and worship leader will incorporate songs into the worship for the day that has to do with the message being preached. One day, during the second summer of this group, I remember seeing a young woman who attended just one time that seemed so beautiful to me. Everyone gathered around her, and I never got a chance to talk to her. I did not want to fall in love while still having these false charges against me.

One of my fondest memories of this group was the time we went camping. About 30 of us went camping and everyone was so nice to each other. I remember camping with old friends who were not Christian and we were never that nice to each other. I remember being thrown into an icy cold lake once by my so-called friends and even trying to throw another guy into a cold river once, but he somehow knocked all four of us down to the ground with his fists and feet.

Another time, we shot fireworks at each other, and still another time we shot each other at point blank with a paintball gun. But this new group of friends was different. One thing we did was break into groups of 6 and then each participated in what they called a cradle of love. 5 of us would pick one person up who was in a laying position. We would rock the person back and forth while saying all kinds of nice things about them. With my eyes closed, while rocking back and forth, I began to cry tears of joy when my new friends covered me with loving compliments.

Chapter 36
"Being a Hypocrite"

The stories I could tell you about what I experienced while preaching on the streets are endless. Each morning I was waking up wondering what exciting thing God had in store for me that day. One thing I realized was that not only was I teaching and preaching to others, but God was teaching me. I seemed to learn a lesson from so many of the encounters I was having. Sometimes I encountered the devil, other times it was my own dark side. Still, other encounters were with angels and even with God himself.

One lesson God taught me was not to take credit for his work in my life. The day I got baptized I asked Jesus to set me free from smoking. The moment I came up out of the water I no longer had a desire to smoke. For forty days, I did not smoke. I was telling everyone that God set me free from smoking. Many people laughed at me for saying this.

Then one day an old friend of mine took me to another old friend of mines' house. The old friend offered me a cigarette. I was excited to tell him I didn't smoke anymore, but then I froze up and didn't continue telling him how Jesus set me free when I got baptized like I was telling everyone else. The Spirit spoke to me and told me to tell him how I got set free. I resisted the Spirit and didn't say anything. Then my old friend asked me how I quit? I told him I just did. He then told me he had tried countless of times to quit and was unsuccessful. He then asked me again how I was able to quit?

The Spirit had told me three times to tell him my testimony about how Jesus set me free. And three times I resisted the Spirit. I think the biggest reason I didn't want to tell him was that I was afraid I would be laughed at. No sooner than the words, "I just quit" left my mouth for the third time, I had the strongest desire to smoke than I had ever had in my life. My voice lowered, and I growled out, "GIVE ME A CIGARETTE!" My old friend threw one at me a little disturbed by my behavior. I think I smoked that cigarette in two or three drags. In no time, it was down to the butt, but I needed more. My eyes were watery from the smoke, my throat hurt from smoking the butt, and I had an unquenchable desire for another cigarette. I couldn't concentrate on anything going on in the room. I looked at my friend and in the still deepened voice said, "Let's get out of here." I needed to get to a gas station and buy a pack of cigarettes.

For the next eight months, I was a smoker again. One day I was at the mall telling kids about Jesus and telling them how he can set them free from smoking. After a little while of telling them about how they could be set free from smoking, I wanted a cigarette myself. So, I decided that I would go and hide behind the mall and smoke a cigarette. While I started walking through the mall, I heard the Spirit call me a hypocrite. I started telling the Spirit that I was not a hypocrite, that a hypocrite is a bad thing, I am doing a good thing by telling these kids how they can be set free from smoking. Just as I was trying to redefine the meaning of the word hypocrite to the Holy Spirit, a young kid around five years old ran past me yelling, "Mommy, mommy, mommy, what's a hypocrite?" What? How come this young kid was asking its mother this question right when I was thinking of the same exact word. I stopped to eavesdrop to hear what the mother had to say. She explained to the child that a hypocrite was someone that was telling other people not to do what they themselves were doing. Bam! The Spirit pinned me to the wall with this experience. I began repeating to myself that I was a hypocrite. As much as I did not like being a hypocrite, I still could not quit smoking yet I wanted to tell people how they could be set free from the addiction.

On one occasion I was downtown during our city's biggest festival called The Cherry Festival, and I saw nothing but people smoking. I usually didn't smoke around anyone who I knew was a Christian, but I didn't see any Christians around. I bummed a cigarette from a guy and then asked him for a light too. He asked if I wanted him to smoke it for me also? After taking just a few drags on the cancer-causing stick, I felt someone tap me on the shoulder while saying my name. I turned around and saw one of the innocent girls from the college-age youth group I was attending. She was saying my name in excitement when she tapped me on the shoulder. When I first turned around she was smiling the biggest smile she could possibly smile. Then out of nowhere, her smile turned into a frown, and she started crying to the point that her lips and body were quivering. I had noticed that her eyes had looked down just before she switched from one extreme emotion to another. She then ran off with one of her friends who was just giving me a cold stare.

I looked down to see what may have caused her to start crying. That is when I realized that it was the cigarette in my hand. I literally felt my heart break when I realized that my smoking hurt this girl.

That night I fell on my knees in my bedroom and cried out to Jesus to set me free again from smoking. I was broken inside. Jesus spoke to me in my broken state and said, "Give me credit." I told him he could have all the credit. I began to beg him to set me free for good, to not let me be enslaved to it ever again. He again said, "Give me the credit". I told him I will, but continued to beg him with all my heart to set me free! He loudly repeated himself a third time in the Spirit and said, "Give me the credit!" I stood up that night a non-smoker.

Chapter 37
"The Smoke Hole"

I started writing single page sermons and would pass them out by hand and pin some up on bulletin boards in the college buildings. At first, I would make just a dozen or so copies and would pass them out. I didn't have much money to pay for copies being I was a full-time student and only had a small part-time job. It was hard to even get 12 people to accept the flyers.

Our city's main high school was butted up to the college grounds that I was attending. Many kids attending the high school would come over to the college woods and smoke cigarettes or just hang out with friends. The kids would get in a lot of trouble if they got caught smoking on the high school grounds, thus the reason they would come over to the college woods. The woods were nicknamed "The Smoke Hole", for obvious reasons.

The Spirit moved me to go to the smoke hole and start passing out my one-page flyers. When I first started handing the flyers out, I could barely get rid of twelve copies of them. Then as the kids started reading them, and became hungrier and hungrier for the word of God, I could not make enough copies. I would have a catchy title on the page, tell an interesting story, then quote some bible verses that pertained to the subject. At first, most kids would crumple up the pages and throw them on the ground. I would humbly go and pick them up, uncrumple them, and hand them to someone else. But when they became spiritually hungry, they had to start sharing the copies. A local church started to make me free copies, but then I was given a key to the copy room in one of the college buildings. I was told that if I needed to make copies that I could go ahead. I worked for the college newspaper and occasionally had to make copies. There was every imaginable color of paper in the copy room. The one who gave me permission to use the copier did not know I was doing what I was doing. I saw it as God making a way for me, and I began making colorful more attractive copies. When you make yourself available, God provides the means you need.

The Smoke Hole was a crazy battleground for souls. One guy stood up on a stump and started saying that God was not real. The Spirit led me to stand up on an even bigger stump and begin to talk about the reality of God. The kid on the smaller stump suddenly looked as though an invisible angel was chocking him. He began choking and gasping for air. He tried to speak again but was not able to. He jumped off of the stump and threw his freshly opened can of pop to the ground.

On one occasion, it was very cold in the Smoke Hole. Someone told me that they hated how cold it was. I looked up to heaven and said, "Wind stop, sun come out!"

To my amazement, the wind instantly stopped, and the sun came out. It immediately felt warmer out. I saw one girl's jaw drop open and eyes widen at what just happened, but a boy said to me that I could see that the sun was going to come out. I agreed with him, as to say he had a point, that maybe I could see that the clouds were about to break, but then I told him I could also see that the wind was about to stop as well. He looked confused. I really could not see that either one was about to happen, I was making a point. We walk by faith, not by sight. I was just as amazed, if not more so, as the others standing around me were that the sun came out and wind stopped right when I told them to.

The scariest experience I had in the Smoke Hole was when a demon began to speak through a boy. While walking down to take my breathalyzer at the police station that morning, I was talking to God about whether the three children who died in the car accident went to heaven or not. God spoke to me and told me that they all made it to heaven. At the very moment that God told me this, the clouds split apart, and an angelic like sunbeam shined down on me, which sent me spiritually soaring. While still floating on cloud nine, I saw Tony the Italian outside putting up letters onto an outdoor sign of the slum hotel. I said hello to him, and he started shaking in his boots. I felt the power of God's Spirit on me so intensely, I figured that Tony had a demon in him that was very uncomfortable around the Spirit that was presently filling me to the max. With the Spirit of God still on me intensely, I walked to the Smoke Hole after I was done taking my breathalyzer to talk to the kids out there that morning. A boy came up to me and started telling me he wanted to talk to me in private. He took me deeper into the woods and then tipped his baseball cap brim down so that I could no longer see his eyes. His voice went very deep, to the point that it was a growl with a snarl. He told me, "they are in hell". I asked him what he was talking about, even though I pretty much already knew what he was talking about.

He then said, "the three kids went to hell". With authority, I told him he was wrong, and that God had just told me they were with him in heaven. He got mad and quickly left me. I was freaked out by the whole incident, but God gave me boldness. I wondered about this boy. I had never remembered seeing him around before this day. I view the encounter this way; if the lying devil is trying to tell me they were in hell, it all the more verified to me that they were not.

A week or so later the boy came out to talk to me again. This time he was carrying a crucifix and a vial of holy water. I asked him what they were for he said his grandmother gave them to him to fight off the demons. I told him that they were not necessary, that he only needed to call on Jesus. He then told me about how he was at some sort of séance the night of the car accident. He said that they saw the accident in the fire they were standing around. He also said he thought he saw one of the kids dragged down to hell. I told him he was deceived.

The next and last time I saw this boy was the best encounter of the three. He said that he went to a youth group service at a church by our mall. The youth pastor had picked up a Bible and told the kids that the Bible is the word of God and that it is the sword of the Spirit. The boy said that when the pastor held the Bible up high in the air, he saw a glowing sword in the pastor's hand. He also said that the demons in the church could not get out of there fast enough when he held up the word/sword. He said demons were flying through the walls of the church. I always found my conversations with this boy very fascinating. He was certainly unique with very unique experiences. I was fascinated that he was able to see the spirit real around us.

Chapter 38
"Visions of Angels"

On two separate occasions, God allowed me to see faces of angels and entire angelic beings. On one of the occasions, I was at a church that liked to sing songs that had very repetitious courses and would blend right from one song to the next. One time during this beautiful praise and worship time at this church, I looked up at the ceiling while singing praises to our Lord and I saw two or three faces made from light looking down through the high school auditorium where this church met. They appeared very pleased at our praising of God. I looked around to see if anyone else could see them. It didn't seem like anyone else could see them. I looked back up, closed my eyes and praised God all the harder. When I opened my eyes again, the faces were gone. I figured it was no different than when someone in the Bible would be allowed to see a glimpse into the spiritual realm, but those around them were not able to see it.

I cherish the moments when God lets me see or hear things that are not of the normal everyday physical realm. It always assures to me that He is more near to us than we often realize. The other occasion where I saw angelic beings was when I had a moment of doubt and wondered if maybe I was the driver of the car during the accident that took the lives of the three children. I believed in my heart that I was not, but at times, I did have doubts being that everyone else seemed to think I was the driver. After all, I had a professional counselor kick me out of rehab because he said I was in such a severe case of denial. It is hard at times to know what the truth is when it seems the entire world is telling you the opposite of what you believe.

Long story short, one day while I was at a church looking out the window facing west, I asked God to show me an angel if I truly was not the driver of the car. When I looked up at the sky, I saw that the clouds had taken on an extra brightness and suddenly transformed into two amazingly huge angelic beings that were facing each other. This vision burned away any doubts I had that maybe my brain was tricking me into believing something that was not true. I now knew beyond a shadow of a doubt that I was not the driver of the car. I only asked God to show me one angel, and he let me see two.

Chapter 39
"Falling in Love"

I did not want to fall in love while I was still going through my ordeal with the court, but when that woman who had attended the college-age youth group just the one time, started attending a bible study I was now leading, I gave in.

I started leading a Bible study at a church that was just down the road from our city's college. It started out very well. We had a lot of high school kids that were also attending it. These were high school aged kids that wanted more spiritual food than they were receiving from the high school aged group they were going to. One day I was called to the church's office by the youth minister and told that he did not want his high school aged daughter and her friends to attend the college-aged bible study. Just then, a bible verse came to my mind, and I felt I should say it, but I resisted.

The verse was about when Jesus told his disciples to not forbid the little children from coming to him. Instead, I just agreed with the youth pastor. After all, he had some good points. He mentioned how I might be going to prison and asked me how he could explain to the parents of the children that I was the leader of the group. He also gave me a scenario where some kids might say they are going to the bible study but then run somewhere else. I believe this youth pastor meant well but was listening to his flesh and to fears instead of seeking God out on this matter. I noticed this a lot with church leaders. They live in fear even though we have not been given a spirit of fear but of power, love and a sound mind.

I regretted not telling the youth pastor the verse that came to my spirit when he was telling me he didn't want the younger kids to come to the group. I felt that I grieved the Holy Spirit by not saying the verse. It hurt even more when I left his office, walked down the hall, and saw a poster I had never noticed before that had a picture of Jesus on it surrounded by children. At the bottom of the poster was the very same verse that I felt I was supposed to say to the youth pastor. Many times, I have fallen short in obeying God. I hate it each time I do. There is indescribable joy when I obey him, and the opposite is true when I disobey.

One of the times I fell short was when I fell in love with the girl I saw only once at the summer college-aged youth group. She wound up coming to the Bible study I was now leading. Come to find out, she only lived a few short miles from me. I invited her to go downtown witnessing with me. She brought a guy that she said was just a friend. As we were at a coffee house praying, I sensed a strong dark presence. Out of the corner of my eye, I could see a satanic throne with the devil himself sitting on it. He appeared in the form of a man dressed in black with his legs crossed while sipping on a hot cup of joe (coffee). I didn't make much out of it at the time, but I did notice the guy she was with was not enjoying himself at all. I am certain he was not a Christian. She loved going out witnessing and wanted to start going out more often. Within no time we were dating. One day, with tears in her eyes, she told me that she lied to me and that she was very sorry. She said the guy she brought with her on our first date was actually her boyfriend but that she was ending it that night.

I forgave her and felt like I won her heart away from the devil himself. Unfortunately, we started getting too much into touching each other. We never made love but might as well have. I remember on one of my first dates with her I excused myself to go use the restroom. While standing at the urinal doing my thing, I heard the Spirit tell me not to touch her. I told the Holy Spirit that I would not, but I didn't last five minutes in keeping my word after I had gotten back to the table. Our hands touched for the very first time, and we held hands it seemed every chance we had after that day. Whenever we kissed, we could not stop until we were completely exhausted. I fell fast, and I fell hard.

Bible study no longer mattered as much. I was about to go to trial and was scared to my core that they were going to find me guilty for a crime I did not commit.

Myself and this woman spent every free second we had together. I often confessed to God that I was sorry for the things we would do together. One time we were in her car at an old abandoned state asylum hospital. We were making out when I saw a dark shadow fly by. It freaked me out. I didn't say anything to her, I just knew I was doing wrong. I was basically trying to escape the hard reality of how unjust the world was by diving into her. I should have been drawing closer to Jesus instead of diving into this woman. Jesus has a way of making life far more bearable. To this day I wonder if things would have turned out differently had I never touched her and kept closer to the Lord. But I have a notion that even though this was not God's perfect plan for me, it was still his plan.

Chapter 40
"Follow Me"

As I said, the stories I could tell you about these spiritual experiences, are endless. I want to tell you more about how I had to go to trial and what resulted with that. But before I do, I feel I need to feed you and encourage you a little. My stories are to help you learn and draw close to Jesus yourself. Once you get well acquainted with him, you are going to have your own stories to tell the people who are still lost in this world. We will overcome the devil by the blood of the lamb and the word of our testimony. If you are at a stage to accept Jesus into your life right now or have already done so and you want to grow more in your faith, then continue reading this chapter. If you are not ready, don't stop reading this story, just skip to the next chapter and read about what the court system did to me. For those of you who are ready, here goes.

The very first step any Christian must do is be born again (get saved). The Bible makes it clear in John chapter 3 that no one can see or enter the kingdom of heaven unless they are born again. Getting into heaven is not about whether or not you lived a good enough life. Every person who has ever walked on the face of the earth, besides Jesus Christ himself, has sinned and is not good enough to get into heaven. You need to have your sins forgiven and need the Holy Spirit in you in order to get into heaven. The Holy Spirit enters you the moment you ask Jesus from your heart and with your lips, to be your Lord and Savior. It is important that you do this from your heart. Many people will call Jesus their Lord on the day of judgement, but he will say "away from me, I never knew you". They confess him as Lord with their mouths, but their hearts are far from him. If you confess with your mouth Jesus is Lord and believe God raised him from the dead in your hearts, you will be saved. Take the first step as soon as you can. Make sure you are saved from going to hell, make sure you are born again.

Once you are saved, and for those who are already saved, you now need to grow up spiritually. You do this by spending time with God (Jesus). Prayer is conversing with God. Talk/Pray to God on a regular basis. Going to a good Bible study will help you grow as well, so does listening to people preach in person, online, or on the radio. Listening to good Christian music helps you grow also. If you do not feed your spirit, you will not grow spiritually. You will remain as a baby in Christ. If you remain as a baby, you won't experience the greater blessings. In order to grow and produce fruit, you must abide in Christ, you must stay connected. Apart from Christ, you will do nothing good spiritually. Seek good Christian fellowship. Other believers will cause you to grow in the Spirit, and you will help them grow as well, just like how iron sharpens iron. Around 2000 years ago

Christ said to pray for the Lord of the Harvest to send out harvesters because the world of souls was ripe. The world is now beginning to rot, and there is a lot of harvesting that still needs to be done. Let's do what we can to bring about an end time revival.

My prayer is that your eyes will be opened, and your heart filled with the love of Christ that he has for this world. He so loved the world that he was willing to die for it. God loves us so much he gave us his only son. His only son had the same deep love as God our Father. They are one and the same. Find out what God's good and pleasing will is, what his perfect personal will for you is. Seek, and you shall find. Do the best that you can to obey God. Any time we deviate and disobey, it stunts our growth and causes pain to us and to others. Connect with the Holy Spirit, listen and obey him. He will lead you to where you need to be, to be all that you can be.

Chapter 41
"Let the Trial Begin"

My trial was a joke. I saw little to no concern for the truth and experienced first hand how corrupt our judicial system can be. I will never forget the day I said to myself if OJ Simpson is found not guilty, they will probably find me guilty. The day I heard that OJ was found not guilty, my heart sank. It made me start to believe that our judicial system is all out of whack.

My eyes really started to open to how bad our judicial system was when I witnessed the jury selection process in my case. One potential jury member was asked if she would do all she could to see that justice was done in my case. She said she would, that it was what God wanted her to do. My attorney called her a loose cannon and wanted to have her dismissed. I told him she was what we wanted and that he should not dismiss her. I felt her heart was in the right place.

The DA, on the other hand, had her dismissed, and my attorney was relieved, I on the other hand was sad. Then there was a state police officer or a retired one, I can't recall. My attorney said that was more like it. I did not see eye to eye with my attorney. The state police in my town seemed corrupt. They had just let one of their own leave the scene of an accident, and later he was allowed to be driven by his wife to the hospital where it was proven he was over the drunk driving limit. But supposedly he went home and drank before going to the hospital, and the test was not an accurate measurement of his alcohol at the time he had crashed into someone else's car. But my attorney insisted on keeping him on the jury. Sometimes I felt my own attorney wanted me to be found guilty more than the DA did.

I could probably write 20 chapters alone on the trial, but I am going to spare you the boring details and give you a summed-up version of it and try to write it in about three chapters. The trial lasted seven or eight days, but so much of the argument was about whether or not I was over the drunk driving limit at the time of the accident, and whether or not it was scientifically possible that I could not remember the accident.

I never did figure out if I was over the drunk driving limit at the time of the accident, both my attorney's witness and the DA's had good arguments one way and the other. I didn't think it even mattered though being that I was not the driver of the car anyways. The actual driver was not over the drunk driving level, which means he couldn't have even be charged with the crime I was being tried for. It also means that the crime I was being tried for had never actually been committed. I was disturbed though that the police were able to confiscate blood that the hospital took for medical testing. Why did the hospital need blood for testing? And if they actually needed it, why would the police take away something they needed? Thinking about it now, it was probably a slick way for the police to get my blood without a warrant. Just have the hospital take it and say it is needed for testing and then if the police need it later it is conveniently available. Most likely the hospital did not need the blood they took from me.

Like I said, I didn't care about what my alcohol level was. The highest they could ever prove it was for sure, was .102, which was probably a half hour after the accident and which showed I hadn't drank very much that night. I hadn't drank nearly enough to have an alcohol-induced blackout. Which leads up to the whole argument about why I couldn't remember the accident. I truly believe I was asleep during the accident and that is why I don't remember anything until after I was awakened by the crash. But they argued for what seemed to be endless hours about whether or not it is possible to not remember a crash.

The DA's witness kept stating he had read every book in the field and never saw an example of someone with this type of traumatic amnesia. He only had a small college degree compared to the witness my attorney called to the stand. Our witness said that he had personally witnessed many cases involving this type of amnesia. He said people bump their heads all the time and can't remember certain events, and that it is different in each case. They argued back and forth about whether or not amnesia in my case was possible. To me this again was a complete waste of time. I was not the driver, what difference did it make why I couldn't remember the crash. I believe it had nothing to do with bumping my head. I had only slept a few hours in the last 48 hours prior to the accident. We had stopped at a park for over a half of an hour. I fell asleep in the passenger's side of the car, pure and simple. They seemed to be making the trial far more complicated then it needed to be. I now wonder if it was a smokescreen for the more pertinent facts that were about to come out. I know for sure one jury member kept falling asleep during the trial and I don't blame him or any others who did. I think I may have as well. The long drawn out testimony of these expert witnesses was extremely boring to the point that it was hurtful to listen to.

I can't recall what order the witnesses were called to the stand, but I remember most of the important testimonies they gave. They called my cousin to the stand who testified that she had seen us leave in my car quite a while before a motorcycle accident happened in our driveway. We didn't have a phone, and a neighbor of ours at the party had to walk home to call the police for the motorcycle accident. We lived out in the country, so our nearest neighbor was a good city block away. After my cousin left the party to go camp down the road on my grandfather's beach, she saw some of the emergency vehicles that were going to the accident I was involved in. This showed that there was at least a good half hour period from the time we left the party to the time we crashed. The motorcycle accident was called in before the accident we were involved in was. The emergency vehicles were in route to our house where the motorcycle accident happened when they were re-routed to the accident I was involved in. It didn't take us over a half hour to drive less than two miles. This proves we did indeed stop at the park by my house. The day after the accident, I had asked the guy who was the actual driver about stopping at the park, and he told me we did not stop. But I thought we had stopped at the park and this testimony by my cousin proved we stopped.

An interesting witness that took the stand was a girl who said she heard the actual driver in the Smoke Hole one day, laughing with friends about how funny it was that they had charged me as being the driver when they didn't know who the real driver was. The DA instantly got mad at her and threatened to put charges on her. She had to get an attorney and plead the fifth the rest of her time on the stand. I briefly talked to her blind mother outside after she testified, and her mom said everything she said was true. This showed me that the DA had the power to shut people up. This didn't settle well with me.

What also didn't settle well with me was how at any time the judge decided to, he would call us into a smaller courtroom to hear people testify in private and then decide what they could or could not testify to in front of the jury, if he would allow them to testify at all. This to me seemed like they were putting on a show for the jury. They would do a practice run in private and then a live act in front of the jury. I felt the jury should be aware of everything, not just shown bits and pieces. Why keep them in the dark about anything unless it is a blatant lie. The most important thing that the jury should not be exposed to are lies. The main witness they were going to call against me was full of obvious lies. Why even pollute the jury with lies? The truth is a narrow thing, but lies are an endless black hole. For Example, my first name is Jash. The truth is, I only have one first name. Now if I wanted to lie, I could give you endless of fake first names. You get the drift.

The main portion of the trial that was used to falsely convict me was based on three main testimonies/evidences;

1. The hair evidence,
2. The lying eyewitness, and
3. Another liar who said he heard me confess to being the driver.

Chapter 42
"Deceiving the Jury"

The DA deceived the jury by using one bogus physical evidence and two lying witnesses. In my mind, you shouldn't even allow a guy who is just pouring out lie after lie to testify, but not only did the judge allow him to testify, he allowed the prosecutor to use him as his star witness. I will just call him Demon. Demon was the only other survivor of the crash other than me. I saw Demon come from the driver's side of the car right after the accident. He crossed from the driver's side of the car, through the car's headlights, and came over to where I was standing in front of the passenger's side of the car. He was literally pulling handfuls of hair from his head while repeatedly saying he had to get out of there. I told him he wasn't going anywhere because his friend needed help. I then began to give his best friend CPR.

Demon was asked by the police who was driving, and he told them that there was a sixth person in the car and that he thinks they were driving but they had run away from the scene of the accident. The police asked me if there was a sixth person in the car. I told them that there was only five. For all I knew, maybe Demon did pick someone else up after I fell asleep, but as you will see later, this was not the case.

After the police found out from me that I didn't know anything about a mysterious sixth person who was the driver, they went and questioned Demon again. This time when they asked him who was driving, he told them he did not know. The police returned to Demon later and informed him that they wanted to take his blood to test his alcohol level in case it was later determined that he was the driver. This was when Demon gave them a third inconsistent statement, a third lie. Demon told them that he thought I was the driver but that he was not sure if I was.

The next day the police visited Demon at his aunt's house and had him call me in the hospital. A police Sergeant was by his side when he called me, and this police Sergeant's daughter was conveniently by my side at the exact same time in my hospital room. This is when I asked him these three important questions;

1. What happened?
2. Didn't we stop at the park? and
3. Didn't I ask if someone else wanted to drive?

He told me I was the driver, that we did not stop at the park, and then hung up on me without answering my last question. That is when Demon turned to the police Sergeant and told a fourth lie. That is when he told the police I was the driver. The Sergeant then wrote in his report stating that Demon said I was the driver. This was

Demon's forth inconsistent statement in regard to who the driver was.

Demon's four inconsistent statements made to the police are as follows:

1. There was a sixth person, I think they were driving.
2. I don't know who was driving.
3. I think Jash was the driver, but I am not sure.
4. Jash was the driver. (Which he didn't tell them until he found out I couldn't remember the car ride).

How much more unreliable can a witness get? On the stand, he testified that he lied to protect me. It wasn't me he was protecting though, it was his own lying butt that he was protecting. You could blame my attorney for not doing a better job at discrediting this witness, but in good faith, the judge and DA should never have even allowed this liar to take the stand and pollute the jury more than they were already polluted by the local media. The local fake news media had polluted the jury's minds for over three and a half years by lying to them countless of times whenever they stated I was the driver as if it was already a proven fact.

A second lying witness the DA called to the stand was one of the paramedics that was at the accident scene. I will call him Liar. All of the other paramedics that were at the accident scene agreed that the only thing I ever said about who was driving, was that I did not know who the driver was. Liar, on the other hand, contradicted them and said that he heard me confess to being the driver. This floored me. I knew I had not said this, and the other paramedics knew I had not said this, but why would someone lie like this? To this day I do not know for sure why he lied. I have a few theories though I would like to tell you.

Mistaken Identification

The most plausible theory I have is; Liar did indeed hear someone confess to being the driver, but it was not me who he heard confess, it was Demon. He testified that I kept telling him to help my friend that was hurt. He also testified that I had a goose egg bump on my forehead. But the funny thing is, I was not friends with the guy who was hurt, Demon was. Funnier yet, I also did not have a goose egg bump on my forehead, but Demon did. Liar testified that it took a lot of milking it out of me, but eventually I told him I was driving. A very interesting fact is that I was not the one Liar took to the hospital. He drove the ambulance that took Demon to the hospital. Why would Liar attend to me at the accident scene but then drive Demon to the hospital? My theory is that Liar heard Demon confess to the crime but had mistaken him for me.

Deal with the DA/Blackmail

Liar was very squirmy while on the stand. If body language says anything at all, his was shouting out that he knew he was lying. But if you give him the benefit of the doubt; the question now is, was he lying on purpose or did he really have a case of mistaken identity? My other theory is, the DA had dirt on Mr. Liar and was making him testify against me in return for some sort of devious trade in favors. The DA did seem pretty desperate, especially since his star witness was a self-admitted liar. Demon testified that his first three statements to the police were lies, but that his fourth statement was the truth. Any logical person would ask, what made his fourth statement any more reliable than his first three? If the DA had dirt on liar or gave him some sort of favor to lie, that is straight up blackmail.

Liar testified that he recognized me because he had seen me drive past him on the highway before. You don't recognize someone by passing by them in the opposite direction at 55 miles an hour. It seemed fishy the way that he said he knew who I was. Demon and I were both 17 years old and both had scruffy hair. Maybe we looked similar to Liar. He testified that he had taken notes the night of the accident but had never turned them into his boss like everyone else did and that he had left his notes in his hotel room.

The only physical evidence that the DA used to falsely convict me of the three 15 year felonies I did not commit, was five invisible to the eye microscopic hair fragments. The police had repeatedly searched the car for physical evidence to try and prove I was the driver. They came up short for over three years. Just before the trial though, they searched the car again and said they found five super small hairs that could not be seen by the naked eye. A woman testified that these hairs proved I was the driver. I will call her Pawn because she may have just been deceived herself and used like a pawn by the DA. I do find it interesting that the FBI recently admitted that they themselves have submitted flawed hair analysis as trial evidence for decades. The FBI admits that the type of hair evidence used in my trial is no longer considered legitimate, that it was used wrongfully for decades. It seems to me, that this hair evidence was used as a last-ditch effort to convict people when they didn't have any other physical evidence against someone.

It seemed suspicious that they found these hair fragments over three and a half years after the accident and just in time for the trial. They said it was because they were so small that it took a lot to find them. The problem is, many people had been in and out of the car, and the hair fragments could have been any number of people's hair. They could have belonged to emergency responders at the scene of the accident, or to someone else who inspected the car. The most ridiculous thing about the hair evidence was the fact that the two pieces found more near the passenger's side were not the same color as Demon's or my hair color.

Pawn testified that they found five microscopic hair fragments on the front windshield. She said three of them were found in the center of the windshield and two were found more near the passenger's side. She testified that the two found more near the passenger's side were more similar to Demon's hair type even though they were not the same color as his hair, and the three found near the center of the windshield were more similar to my hair type. They could only compare similarities; they could not conclude with certainty that they were one person or another person's hairs, and they never tested anyone else's hair that was in the vehicle before, during, or after the accident.

Even though this evidence at face value was very flimsy, Pawn, with the help of the DA, did a great job misleading the jury into believing it was legitimate. They talked about how the windshield was cracked indicating we hit our heads into it. They talked about how both Demon and I had head injuries. They even went as far as to redefine physics and say that even though none of the forces during the crash would have projected the front seat passengers forward into the windshield, that we defied the laws of physics and magically flew forward into the windshield anyways. They said we were like ping pong balls in a jar, and we must have bounced into the windshield even though all the rest of the physical evidences reveals that we never flew in that direction.

Chapter 43
"The Better Legitimate Evidences"

The better and more legitimate evidences that came forth in my trial were the evidences that did not defy physics, were not misleading and proved who the real driver was. They were presented by two individuals who testified, not just on behalf of me, but on behalf of the truth. One was an accident reconstructionist who reconstructed the accident, and the other was a paramedic who explained the injuries Demon sustained during the accident.

The accident reconstructionist, who I will call Angel, explained in super fine detail every force that was involved in the accident. He explained every direction the car flew, as well as the direction each passenger flew in the car. Angel explained how he knows all of this because of the known sustained injuries to the passengers and the known sustained damage to the car. He said it was called "Place matching evidences". He said for example, in a head-on crash, you know the passengers are thrown forwards in a car. He testified that often in a head-on crash, there will be damage sustained to the steering wheel, and the driver will sustain an injury to his chest. In a case like a head-on crash, the known sustained injury is the chest injury, and the known sustained damage to the vehicle, is the damaged steering wheel; that is how place matching evidence works. The chest injury matches the damaged steering wheel. The paramedic, who I will call Saint, testified and explained that he recalled the injuries Demon had sustained during the accident and that he had also filled out a medical form that indicated these injuries. Saint showed us the form that indicated Demon's injuries and explained to us what he had written on it (See Included Medical Documents). Demon had sustained a significant injury to his right shoulder. At first, they thought Demon's shoulder was dislocated. Demon also sustained quite a good size bump to his forehead. These two physical injuries that Demon sustained proved he was the actual driver during the accident.

Let me explain how Demon's two injuries proved he was the driver. Angel testified that the driver of the car would have at first been thrown up and slightly forward, not directly forward into the windshield like a person would be thrown in a head-on crash, but up into the upper portion of the windshields' trim. Angel said this force was caused when the car first left the road, started sliding sideways and then hit the first smaller tree that catapulted the car into the air while flipping it. He said the force was even backed up by the physical concaved dent that was in the windshield's trim. He said the dent was obviously made from a head striking it and that the driver is the one who impacted this trim.

Demon's forehead injury was caused by impacting the windshield's trim. It is a black and white place matching evidence that puts Demon in the driver's seat at the time of the accident. His **forehead injury** was the known **sustained injury,** and the **concaved dent** in the windshield's trim was the known **sustained damage** to the vehicle. But wait, there is more.

After the car left the first tree, it began to roll over sideways high in the air. As it was rolling, it impacted a much larger tree which caused it to fly in a different direction until it landed on the ground. Angel explained how the damage to the car and the two trees the car hit, the injuries sustained by the passengers, and the marks on the road, all proved the way that the car flew around during the crash. He was very good at his job. Too bad my attorney was not.

The way the car spun after hitting the second tree threw the car's passengers backwards with an incredible force. Two of the back-seat passengers were thrown out the rear window. The driver was thrown back into the driver's seat. Angel went into great detail about how the driver was thrown back into the driver's seat with an incredible force. He said the damage sustained to the driver's seat proved this. He said the driver's seat was bent back 18 inches in the right shoulder area, and that it had to be a great impact because of the steel rod that was bent in the seat. It takes a lot of force to bend a steel rod like the one in the driver's seat.

Wow! I was super excited when Angel had explained that the driver of the car damaged the right shoulder area of the driver's seat because Demon had a matching injury. The known sustained injury that Demon sustained was a **right shoulder injury**, along with his forehead injury. The known sustained damages were the **damaged right shoulder area of the driver's seat** and the dent in the windshield's trim. Saint had testified that Demon had injured both his forehead and right shoulder pretty severely during the accident.

I got excited and tried to tell my attorney who didn't want to listen to me at the moment. He was busy trying to figure something out. After Angel was dismissed, I told my attorney that this proved Demon was the driver and I wanted him to explain it to the jury who didn't seem to understand. By the jury's lack of response, it appeared that they had not pieced together Angel's testimony with Saint's testimony. My attorney told me that he did not want to bring back up evidences or witnesses that the jury already saw and listened to. What? It all goes back to my attorney telling me it was not his job to prove my innocence. He told me it was the DA's job to prove me guilty and that his job was just to poke holes in the DA's case.

My attorney thought he had already poked enough holes in the DA's case. I kept thinking to myself, what better hole could we poke than prove my innocence? But my attorney would not elaborate on the place matching evidences. I felt we needed to poke a bigger hole because of how polluted the jury was by the media for over three and a half years. Maybe it wouldn't have mattered if we poked a hole the size of the state of Texas in the DA's case.

What was one day of good evidence against a thousand days of the fake media's lies? In my mind, the judge and DA should have at least been able to see the truth, and maybe they did, but just didn't care. For the most part, the judge often didn't seem to even pay that close attention to what the witnesses were saying. Maybe this was a result of the first witnesses who bored us to death with all their talk about whether I was over the drunk driving limit or whether I really suffered amnesia. In any case, I felt I was living in a nightmare. The court system looked completely pathetic to me at this point.

Chapter 44
"The Verdict"

My attorney must have gotten the bad news before it was publicly made known because his entire demeanor changed. He was very optimistic at first that I would be found not guilty, but now he asked me in a less positive sounding voice, "What if it doesn't go the way I thought?" I didn't ever really have his optimistic view of the trial anyways. He was horrible at his job, and the DA used too many lies to deceive the jury, and the judge allowed it all to happen. I felt like they were all against me, but worse than that, I felt they were all against the truth and against justice. Truth and justice are the very core things the judge and DA should be most concerned about.

It did not take the jury long to come back with their verdict. They came back with a guilty verdict on all charges. It crushed my heart. I told my dad it was a miracle.

My dad said it was not a miracle, but the opposite of a miracle. I called it a miracle because I didn't think it was possible to prove beyond a shadow of a doubt to 12 people that someone did something they really did not do. Even though I had first hand experience of how messed up our judicial system was, and even though I was not optimistic like my attorney was, I still had a sliver of hope that the DA didn't completely convince 12 people of a lie, that maybe one of them saw the light of truth through the smoke screen of darkness and lies. I had taken the stand myself, and so did Demon, but they didn't seem to care what I had to say, and they didn't care that Demon was telling even more lies. While testifying, Demon changed his story and contradicted himself by saying we may have stopped at the park, and that we may have spent time together making up lies to tell the police before anyone arrived at the accident scene.

Demon's testimony was a joke. All it really took though was him pointing the finger at me again and saying it was me who was driving not him. It was my car after all, but legally I was not allowed to drive after 11pm at night because of my driving curfew. I almost religiously let other people drive my car after 11pm because I didn't want to get caught breaking the law. I wish I drove that night. I believe the three kids would still be alive today if I had.

I hate the fact that I even let my car on the road that night. I hate that I gave into the peer pressure of the kids begging me for a ride.

My dad told me not to go anywhere that night, but I disobeyed my dad when the kids would not stop asking me for a ride. I thought their car was only a half mile from my house. I never would have imagined this would be what came from doing something that I thought was a good thing. I thought it was bad to disobey my dad, but thought I was doing a good thing for the kids that so desperately wanted to get to their car. I was willing to hurt my relationship with my dad to help these children. Instead, my relationship grew better with my dad, and the children wound up dead. What a nightmare it all was.

Chapter 45
"My Sentencing"

After being found guilty, I was allowed to leave the courtroom and remain on bond. My sentencing date was around a month away. I didn't know what to do. I still wanted to prove my innocence even though the media was now really burying their hatchet. How do you convince society of something when everyone is being brainwashed into believing the exact opposite? I ran to every pastor I could, and anyone else who might listen and might be able to help. Most of them wanted to help me get a small sentence. I didn't care so much about a lenient sentence; I should not be the one getting any sentence at all. People started saying they would write the judge and DA for me to request that they go light on me. This just made me think people did not get it. They did not know what type of injustice they just witnessed in their town. To throw a man in prison for something he did not do is unjust! Not punishing the actual guilty person is unjust as well!

My girlfriend and I spent as much time as we could together. I felt strongly about marrying her, and I know she felt the same towards me, but having this unknown amount of time apart in our near future, scared us both. We remained as pure as we could, we both wanted to wait until we were married to do anything sexual. There were days that I was weak though and thought I was going to fall, but she was strong those days. And there were days she was weak, but I was strong. We thanked God that there was never a day we were both weak at the same time.

One day my fiancée suggested that we walk up to the church by my house. It was night time, but this church always left its doors open. We went in and prayed. I looked around, and I found a keyboard to play with. While we were there, a priest walked in. My fiancée suggested we go talk to him. He took us into a back room, and we talked. I explained to him what I was going through and he suggested that I should lie and say I did it. I told him that that was not what God wanted me to do, that God kept telling me to tell the truth and that even the Bible says we should tell the truth.

He got mad at me and told me sometimes it is better to lie. I understand that sometimes it is, but I didn't see how it was better to lie in my case, and besides, God was telling me not to. In my mind, the best thing for everyone was to tell the truth. The best thing would be to make Demon stand trial and reveal the truth by proving he was the actual driver. I especially felt bad for the families of the deceased. I believed that they deserved to know the truth more than anyone else. Everyone was lying to them. I didn't think it was right for me to lie to them also. I was disappointed that the priest wanted me to lie when God so strongly was telling me to tell the truth.

My fiancée didn't like how the whole talk went with the priest. Looking back now, I wonder if she had set the whole meeting up with him. She did seem to be crafty at things like that. She once had me invite a guy out with us after bible study while she invited a girl to come along also who liked this guy. I know she was just playing matchmaker, with the two college kids, who by the way wound up getting married, but it never felt right to me to do things this way. It felt like a form or deception.

Just before my sentencing date, I was called into my attorney's office. He started telling me what I had to do at sentencing. He said I had to show remorse, and that if I could shed some fake tears, it would help. He informed me that the families of the deceased would be in the courtroom and that I needed to also say I was the driver. I did not feel right about looking the deceased's family members in their eyes while lying to them. I told my attorney that I was not going to lie. I informed him that I was not the driver and that God knows I was not. My attorney went satanic on me at this point. He told me he did not care what me and my God knew really happened, that I needed to lie and say I was the driver or else I was going to go to prison. He then told me that the judge was my god now.

What in the world was my attorney talking about? I couldn't believe what was coming out of his mouth. As far as I knew, this man went to church every Sunday and had some sort of faith in God, but why would he ever say that the judge was my god now, and why would he call God, "my God", instead of our God? He said it as if we served different gods. I now saw my attorney as being as far from God as a man could get because he was telling me to do the exact opposite of what God was telling me to do. I almost wonder at times if he took a bribe to help get me convicted. There were times when I felt the DA was doing a better job at bringing out my innocence than my own attorney was. The DA was the one who asked most of the questions that showed Demon had injuries that proved he was the driver. It was the DA's cross-examination of our own witness that brought most of the truth out in my case.

It now made sense to me why my attorney had me hide my Bible whenever I brought it into the courtroom. I thought he didn't want the jury or judge to see it, but now I think he himself couldn't stand looking at it. I loved that the court made me swear before God to tell the truth, the whole truth, and nothing but the truth, so help me God. I said, "I do" with a smile on my face. Demon also had to say the same swearing-in oath before he testified against me. I don't think God was pleased with Demon swearing before him to tell the truth, only to bear false witness against me. Before I was sentenced, I had to go see a lady and do a presentencing interview with her. I first had to fill out a form in the lobby and then wait to meet with her. I filled out most of the form and then decided to read the Bible while I waited. I was fascinated with how the Bible was so relevant in my day to day life. I couldn't get enough reading of it, and took it everywhere I went. When the presentencing lady called me in to meet with her, she scolded me for not completely filling out the form I was given. She said I could have been filling out the rest of the form instead of reading the Bible. I humbly explained to her that I did not understand what some of the questions on the form were asking me, and I didn't want to fill it out wrong. She also seemed very negative towards the Bible. It was mainly how the demeaning tone in her voice was when she said "the Bible".

The day came when I had to be sentenced. I stood before the families of the deceased and told them I was not the driver. This did not go over well with them, my attorney, or the judge. The judge started calling me names that I didn't even know the meaning of. The families scolded me and said I still would not admit to what I did. Then the judge told me I was being sentenced to one year in the county jail and to five years of probation. He then explained a few other things I had to do during those five years. Then they took me away in handcuffs. I heard a number of screams and crying in the courtroom. One person that I know for sure that was crying, was my girlfriend. I told her it would be alright. I was fearful that I was going to get sentenced to 45 years in prison. I was charged with three felonies that each carried a sentence of up to 15 years in prison, but apparently each crime would be served simultaneously. This meant that the most time they could sentence me to was 15 years. None-the-less, one year didn't sound like very long to me. It was the five years of probation that sounded like a lot longer amount of time. I had already done nearly four years on a bond that was very burdensome.

Chapter 46
"County Jail"

I was given credit for the 10 days that I had initially served when I was first charged with the crimes, and with good time, I was only going to have to spend 10 months in the county jail. To no longer be on bond was a relief to me. It was very stressful being on bond. Anytime I missed a breathalyzer or drug test, they threatened to take away my bond. Sometimes I would run to the state police post or the hospital to take a breathalyzer or drug test if I was late getting to the one I was supposed to take at the police station. This would prove I did not miss them because I had been drinking or doing drugs.

One time they did make me spend a weekend in jail because I missed a drug test on Thanksgiving Day. I was helping pass out food at a church and forgot all about taking a drug test that day. I felt far less stressful now that I did not have to worry about messing up my bond. The jail had some good religious services that I liked to attend, and I now had plenty of time to read the Bible. I spent a lot of time writing my girlfriend, who actually became my fiancée while I was in the county jail. I proposed one day while on the phone with her. The worst part about the county jail was that you were bored out of your mind. You were pretty much stuck in a small six to sixteen-man cell for 23 to 24 hours a day. My fiancée visited me each week, and we were growing deeper in love now that we were not tempted to fornicate at all. It all seemed good until I met with my probation officer. He said that he had a probation order that I needed to sign. I looked at the probation order and couldn't believe how much was being required of me. I told him that there must have been a mistake, that the judge didn't say I had to do half the stuff that was written on this probation order. I figured that the judge ordered that I do some of the stuff, but the probation officers must have added a lot more requirements to it because it was now an insane amount of stuff.

I asked my probation officer if he had ever seen a probation order like this before, he said it happens. I asked him again if he personally had ever seen one like this. He reluctantly admitted that he had not. I was only going to be allotted three to five hours of sleep a day for the next five years. I told him I would try my best to do all that they were asking me to do, but I could not sign it because I would be lying if I signed it stating that I would completely comply to all of the requirements. I said I wanted to meet with the judge to try and clear this up. I figured that there must have been a mistake.

I had also written the judge and asked him what I should be doing with my time in jail. He told me to seek the forgiveness of God and the family members of the deceased. I knew God had already forgiven me for the role I had played in the deaths of the children, but I knew the family members were still angry, so I began to write the family members. I tried my best to tell them how bad I felt for the role I played but that I felt they deserved to know the truth. I think I wrote them each three letters. Instead of mailing the letters all out at once I planned on mailing them a few days apart.

Shortly after mailing the first letter to the families, I was told by my probation officer that he did not think it was a good idea for me to contact the family members. But the judge was the one who told me to seek the forgiveness of the family members, so I continued to do what the judge told me to do. Then the probation officer met with me again and said I was to stop sending them letters.

Soon after my probation officer told me to stop writing forgiveness letters to the families of the deceased, I met with the captain of the jail and asked him whether my probation officer had more authority than the judge. The captain told me that the judge had more authority. Which is what I thought, so I continued to obey the judge.

I figured the only way my probation officer even knew I mailed the letters was because the jail told him when they saw the letters I was mailing out, so I put the last letters I wrote in a big manila envelope and sent them out to my fiancée. She picked them up from the jail and then mailed the last letters for me. Then I received a new copy of my probation order from my probation officer. Added to the probation order was a new condition that stated, I was to have no contact with the families of the deceased. I tried calling my fiancée to stop her from mailing the last letters, but she was not home. When I did get a hold of her, she told me she had already mailed them. I figured that it didn't really matter because they were written and sent out before I actually had this new probation stipulation. Besides this, a probation order is not even in effect until after a person is released from jail. The five years of probation I was sentenced to was not to begin until I was released from the jail.

I then had my probation officer's boss come visit me. He instantly started yelling at me about how we were not friends and something about how do I explain guys who read the Bible but like to look at baby boy's butts? I had no idea where this guy was coming from, why he was so angry, and why he was saying the things he was. He seemed posed by demons to me.

Whoever said anything about being friends, and I never said anything about the Bible to him. He was a very strange man. He told me I was getting my wish and that I would get to meet with the judge soon. I was excited yet confused. He informed me that it was the judge who added the new stipulation to my probation, about not contacting the families of the deceased. This did not make sense to me. Why would the judge tell me not to contact the very people he told me to contact and seek the forgiveness of? I prepared for my meeting with the judge. I tried my best to write up a weekly schedule to show him how impossible the probation order was. My probation officer had told me I would have to work a full-time night job because during the day I had to take a breathalyzer, work with M.A.D.D., take drug tests, go to AA meetings and other counseling classes. I was told I would have to do so many hours a year working with M.A.D.D. I asked if I could do all the hours first and get them over with so that I could then get a full-time job, but he told me I would have to work with M.A.D.D. during the day and only so many hours a week and that was why I would need a night job. I asked him, if this is the case, when was I supposed to sleep if I had to take a breathalyzer in the morning, work with M.A.D.D. and go to classes during the day, go to A.A. in the evenings and work a full-time night job. He said it was not his problem and that the DA had an appeal in to get me re-sentenced to prison anyways and that it looked like I was going to prison for violating my probation.

What? How did I violate my probation that was not even going to start for another six or seven more months? He said that the letters were the last straw with the judge. I still didn't understand why the judge was so mad at me for writing and asking the families of the deceased to forgive me when it was what he that told me to do it in the first place. Besides that, I did not write and mail any letters after I was notified about the new stipulation that was added to my probation order. How could they punish me for something I did before it was illegal for me to do it? The letters were written and mailed before there was a new stipulation added to my probation order. At the worst, my fiancée mailed them out the same day they added a new stipulation to my probation order. I tried to call her and stop her, but she was unreachable.

While I was still in the county jail, a woman from a local rehabilitation center came and interviewed me before all the probation order stuff went down. I will call her Tree. She came and interviewed me and said she could get me out of jail sooner if I qualified for rehab. Because of my last experience with rehab, I didn't want anything to do with it again. She informed me that the rehab center she worked for was better than the other one that I had got kicked out of, and she said that I would like hers. I told her about my getting saved experience and about how God had written my name in the sky.

She informed me that she didn't believe I had a drinking or drug problem but that she was going to tell the judge I did to get me out of jail sooner. I didn't like the fact that she wanted to lie to the judge and I certainly didn't give her permission to. She will come back into the picture later in my story. I also received a letter from Demon's mother while still in the county jail. The only part of her letter that I remember was her asking me, "Where is your God now?" I shrugged it off because I believed God was still where he always is. God was still at the same place he was when this cruel world killed his only son Jesus; God was still on his throne. I understand she was trying to add to my pain by kicking me while I was down and make me doubt God's goodness, but my faith was rock solid in God, it was humanity I was losing more and more faith in. It just made me see her as a wicked person for doing this.

Chapter 47
"Resentencing"

My meeting with the unjust judge wasn't at all what I had hoped for. I had hoped that the judge would see that the probation order was not realistically possible for a person to do. It demanded too much from a person. There was a good chance that the probation order was a set up. Meaning, that I was not supposed to be able to obey it all, and that way, the judge could resentence me at any time he wanted to during the next five years of my life.

Where it really became a set up was when he added that I was to have no contact with the families of the deceased, but at the same time, he was ordering me to work with M.A.D.D. for 400 hours a year. I had heard that the mothers of the three deceased were part of M.A.D.D.. How was I supposed to work with them but at the same time, have no contact with them?

When I stood before the judge, who I will refer to as Heartless, he told me I had made the biggest mistake of my life. I said what, "Getting a court-appointed attorney?" He said the mistake was writing the parents of the deceased. I told him I was only doing what he had told me to do. Heartless told me that I was supposed to go through the court, not write them on my own. This was so wrong! He never said anything about going through the court. He simply told me to seek the forgiveness of God and of the families. Was I also supposed to go through the court to seek God's forgiveness also?

The judge said that I was being re-sentenced for violating my probation. The probation officer told me that even though I had not signed the probation order agreeing to it, that it did not matter, I was still bound to it. He also said that by not signing it, I was basically saying I would not obey it. I reminded him that I told him I would try my best to obey it, but I could not sign it simply because no one could possibly obey all that it required. No one can live off three to five hours of sleep a day for five years and not mess up a little. I doubt I would have even lasted a month. This was just another level in their twisted and demented game they were playing with me. If they really cared about the families of the deceased, they would have tried harder to tell them the truth instead of perpetuating the lie they started the day they charged me for a crime I did not commit.

Judge Heartless, then re-sentenced me to the amount of time that the DA was appealing to the higher courts asking them to force him to sentence me to; which was 6-15 years in prison. For all I know, the DA would have won a second time appealing another one of Heartless' rulings, and I would have been re-sentenced 6 months after being on probation anyways. The whole system seems messed up to me. And this is just the tip of the iceberg. I had hoped that it was just the small rinky-dink court system in my town that was so wicked, but as I discovered, it goes much further than just the lower local court levels.

Chapter 48
"Quarantine"

The most time you could do in a county jail was one year, now that I was sentenced to 6-15 years; I had to go to the big house, to prison, to the Michigan Department of Corrections (M.D.O.C.). The sentence didn't seem that much different to me than having to do one year in jail and then 5 years on probation. Either way they were planning on controlling my life for the next 6 years. I don't know how it is even legal to make someone work for a hate-based organization like M.A.D.D., like they were trying to make me do. As far as I understood, M.A.D.D. was planning for me to go and do talks at the schools around my town and tell all the kids how dangerous drunk driving was and lie and tell the kids I killed three kids while drunk driving. Basically, I was not just being asked to lie to the families of the deceased, but also to all of the children around my town. Anyhow, prison seemed like it was going to be a relief. At least now I was not going to be asked to lie to people; so I thought anyways.

When you first get sent to prison, you must go to quarantine. I had two local transportation officers drive me down to Jackson Michigan to the oldest and biggest prison in The United States. On the way there, one of the officers kept trying to harass me, but the other one stopped him. One thing the officer said to me was that I better look at the women now because I am not going to see any for a long time. I told him I was engaged and didn't need to look at other women. He laughed at me and started to say something about her leaving me, but that was when the other officer stopped him. We then picked up another inmate that they were transporting back to my city after dropping me off. The inmate asked me if I was scared. I told him God was with me. As we pulled into the parking lot of the prison a song called "Welcome to the Jungle" was blaring on the radio. The devil tried to make me scared by using this song and its devilish lyrics, but God had strengthened my heart, and I was able to remain bold.

I was disturbed by what next I had to go through. I was put in a holding cell that had a toilet in the middle of the room where everyone would see you using it. Then I had to strip down and shower in front of people including inmates, and both male and female guards. It was pretty humiliating and humbling.

You basically had to remain naked until you were called up to a quartermaster window to receive your prison clothes. Privacy was completely gone. The next thing to go was my first name. In prison, they make your last name your first name and give you a number as your last name. My name became "Lardie 255916". I was breathless when I arrived at the cell block I was going to be staying in. It was a big, long as the eye can see hall, with five stories of small cells staked up on each other on both sides of the hall. They called them bird cages and the name fit. It looked like men were put in bird cages five stories up. I just stood there staring at it in amazement. Next to me sat an old black man who couldn't stop laughing because of the look on my face. They sent me to my cell and locked me in. It was nice to finally be in a cell by myself, but there were so many people around that you could hear but just not see. It was just like in a movie; the clanging sound of the doors opening and closing, the yelling of inmates, the guards constantly walking by your cell. The back of the cells had a catwalk so that guards could walk both in front of your cells and behind. The cells' walls were completely open in the front and back except for bars. The side walls were made of cinder blocks.

One of the worse experiences I had while in quarantine was taking a shower. It was an open bay type of shower. I think there were twenty guys all trying to shower with only half as many shower heads. You basically had to take turns getting wet and rinsing off. You would get wet, step out of the way without bumping into another naked man, soap up, then wait till there was an opening to rise off. I was the only white guy in the shower, and a lot of guys were staring at me. Needless to say, I only took one or two showers in the three weeks I was there. It didn't help that you had to be 21 years old to go to the adult quarantine, which was how old I was. This meant that I was the youngest you could be at this prison. Prison is not a good place for anybody, but it is especially not a good place for a young white kid. I was suddenly a minority. I thank God that He, God, was with me. He promises to never leave us or forsake us. A prisoner told me I should just take bird baths in my sink with a washcloth. Another prisoner said that if I do go to the showers, and I drop the soap, just kick it away from me. He said, whatever you do, don't bend over to pick it up. I could tell that he was not joking but had really meant what he said.

I was appointed another attorney to represent me in my appeals. I met with him while in quarantine for the first time. I explained to him that I was innocent of the crimes they found me guilty of. He said he didn't care that I was innocent. I asked him why no one cared that I was innocent. He got mad at me and said it was because I was a dope smoking, drinking teen! As soon as he finished saying this, I thought God was striking him dead. He began gasping for air and then started grabbing his chest. He then pulled an inhaler out of his shirt pocket and took a big drag or two off it.

I hadn't smoked or drank anything in years, and I was now in my twenties. The accident happened when I was 17, but now I was 21 years old. And I always believed in the motto "With liberty and justice for all!" I felt the same laws should apply for a dope smoking, drinking teen as they do for anyone else. My attorney said he didn't see any grounds for an appeal but that he felt I got sentenced to too much time, so he was going to try for a time reduction. I didn't care about the time I was sentenced to as much as I did about getting my name cleared. I saw all types of grounds for an appeal, I just didn't know how to legally articulate them. I mainly saw the three bogus pieces of evidence they used to falsely convict me as being the best grounds for appealing on.

The saddest part about quarantine was how many people were killing themselves. At least once a day the lights would begin flickering on and off while making a strange buzzing and electric crackling sound. I thought it was sort of neat until I was informed by another inmate that it was from guys electrocuting themselves. I remember that shortly after the lights did this one time, I saw a golf cart type mobile, that looked like a small pickup truck, drive by with a body covered with a sheet on it. Many of the guys around me had just been sentenced to some very long sentences, some had even gotten life sentences.

Personally, the saddest thing that happened while I was in quarantine was my grandmother killing herself. In quarantine, you get one hour of time in the prison yard. It was a small fenced-in prison yard. It is the only time that you have to use a phone. I had talked to my grandmother, and she sounded very sad. She told me she believed in me and to remember that, no matter what happens. That was the last time I talked to her. A few days later my fiancée told me my grandmother had purposely driven her car at a high speed off of a dead-end street.

Chapter 49
"TCF"

I was shipped out of quarantine and sent to a prison called "Thumb Correction Facility" (T.C.F.). It was located in the thumb area of our state around 175 miles from my city. Which was about a three and a half hour drive.

They mostly only call a prison by its initials. TCF was a more relaxed prison. It still had its dark side, but it was the closest prison our state had to a country club. It had two tennis courts, four basketball courts (one indoor, three outdoor), horseshoe pits, shuffleboard slabs, handball courts, a volleyball court, two weight pits (one indoor, one outdoor), a nice figure eight paved track, and two baseball diamonds. Not to mention each living unit had four big screen color television rooms, a big game\card room, as well as vending machines filled with drinks and snacks.

I was given a key and taken to a two-man cell and soon met my first bunky (roommate). He seemed very nice at first. He offered me some tobacco, and I accepted some. I smoked one cigarette, and it felt like a dark spirit had grabbed me by my throat. For the next three days, I wanted to smoke some more, but I repeatedly cried out to Jesus to help me resist the temptation to smoke anymore and apologized to him for smoking the one. Jesus gave me the strength to not get addicted again to smoking. I couldn't believe how much time we got to spend outside; it was around ten hours a day. My first day in this prison, I tried to play basketball. That was when I discovered that white men can not jump. They had the shortest non-white guy covering me. He was at least a foot shorter than me, but he could jump a foot higher than me. One time he jumped up and blocked four of my shots in a row. The other players were almost rolling on the ground from laughing so hard. I never again tried to play a basketball game in prison.

I rode into this prison with three other guys. I was not black like them, but two of them saw beyond my color and accepted me as their friend. The three of us would eat in the chow hall together, and I hung out with these two pretty regularly. At least I did up until my eyes were opened to one of the dark realities of prison.

One day a young white kid asked me if I was a punk (homosexual). I told him that I was not. He then asked me why I hung out with only black guys. He also asked me if I ever noticed that all the white guys, except punks, sat together in the chow hall. I thought the whole prison was basically black, but I guess maybe it is only 80 percent. The next time I was in the chow hall I looked over to the one area and for the first time noticed that all of the whites sat together, and there was even another chow line that the whites used. I was floored to find out how blind I was and couldn't believe that prison was segregated by its own free choice. The three guys I always ate with saw how confused and sad I was. They told me it was ok and that I could go sit with the whites. I think I almost cried when I got up from their table and walked over to the other area of the chow hall. I left my only friends and went to sit with complete strangers, just because of skin color.

I still hung out with one of the three black guys. We went to church together, and he talked me into joining the choir. I was the only white guy in the choir, but in the church services, the color of your skin was not an issue. The only time I ever really felt out of place while in the choir was when we sang some songs for the Kwanzaa celebration at the prison. Kwanzaa is an African heritage celebration. For Kwanzaa, I found myself in a gymnasium with hundreds of inmates in it, and only two of us were white. To say the least, I did not sing a solo that day.

My bunky told me not to sign up for the church services at this prison. He told me the only guys that attended the services were baby rapers. I was beginning to not trust my bunky because of some of the things he was saying and the way he was acting. I was scared to go to church services at first because of what he had said, but was so glad once I started going. There were some really good and decent men in the church services. My bunky, on the other hand, went demonic on me. One night he began punching the bottom of my bunk repeatedly while yelling "Die Christian, Die!" He also started calling me a "fish" as if this term was supposed to hurt me. He told me that a fish is someone who is brand new to prison. He told me to look out the window and read the three letters on the hillside. I could see "T.C.F." in big letters on the hillside by the helicopter landing pad. He said the letters stood for "Turkey, Chicken, Fish" and that I was a fish. He went on to explain that a turkey was someone that was telling on other people and a chicken was a person who was afraid and needed extra security. He said that these three types of people were the only ones they put in this particular prison. I wondered to myself which of these three things my bunky was. It was obvious he was not a fish.

My bunky then played the role of a turkey and reported me to the prison guards. He told on me for giving another inmate some food. In prison, you are not technically allowed to give food to other inmates that you buy from the commissary (prison store). A prison guard called me into the office and said he understood that I was a Christian, and that because I was, I wanted to feed those who were hungry. He then told me that it was not allowed, and that these were not my neighbors. He informed me that it causes people to get taken advantage of and that it would be wiser for me to not get caught up in such a mess. I was then moved into a different cell with a different inmate. The officer was right about not giving food away. It was also not wise to accept food from people you didn't know. I had accepted a can of pop from an inmate I didn't know in the first few days I had arrived at this prison. The guy later started telling me I had to pay him back right away. He was about to try to make me repay him with a sexual favor, but an older white guy went and threatened to kill him. I couldn't understand why this old guy stood up for me, but I thanked God that he did. The elderly white guy told me he just didn't like seeing young white guys taken advantage of. He also told me he was already doing life in prison so it didn't matter if he were to kill someone.

My second bunky was an ex-state trooper (police officer). I had a homosexual prison guard that started coming around my cell which made me feel very uncomfortable. I think he might have intended on raping me, but my new bunky began screaming at him one day and he never came around again. I couldn't believe this inmate was yelling at one of our prison guards, because you can get in a lot of trouble for doing so, but I was glad that he did.

I spent two years at this prison and could probably write an entire book on just these first two years, but I will just mention the more relevant parts. After a year of sticking by my side, my fiancée left me. She would drive three and a half hours to come see me once a week for a year, spend all day with me, and then drive three and a half hours back home. When other inmates found out what I was about, they began giving me all kinds of religious pictures. I completely covered my bulletin board with pictures of Jesus. As time went on, I started replacing all the pictures of the Lord with pictures of my fiancée. Each visit we were on, we would get two Polaroid pictures taken, one for her and one for me. Before long, my whole day was consumed with my fiancée. If I wasn't writing letters to her, I was on the phone with her or on a visit with her. If I wasn't writing or talking to her, I was just laying around thinking about her, dreaming of what life was going to be like once I was free.

Then one day while taking a shower I heard God tell me that he was about to take away the apple of my eye. The Bible talks about a guy who God told this to just before God killed his wife. I begged God not to kill her. I honestly was scared she was going to die. I didn't see any other way she would leave me at this point other than dying because we were so madly in love with each other. A few days after hearing from God in the shower, I was laying on my bed looking at all the pictures I had of my fiancée on my bulletin board, and I heard God tell me I had turned her into an idol. I tried arguing with God and told him I still had one picture of him in the center of my bulletin board. I told him this meant He was still in the center of our relationship. Just then, while I was still conversing with God, an inmate opened my cell door, pointed at the last picture of Jesus on my bulletin board, and told me he wanted to borrow the picture, so he could paint it. I said "No"! But this inmate began to get mad and began to beg me for it. I reluctantly took it down and gave it to him. How could I not. After all, this guy was one of, if not the biggest, guy in this prison. He was Italian and had been stabbed repeatedly for trying to save the life of another Italian when he first got locked up. After his near death experience, he spent most of his time in the weight pit. He told me he was in prison for killing a guy who had 666 tattooed on his neck. He said he figured he was just sending the guy to meet the one he served.

As soon as the monsterous inmate left my cell, I heard God say, "Where am I now?" As I was staring at the empty hole in the middle of my bulletin board. I tried to replace the picture with a different one, but none of the other pictures were the right size and didn't look right.

The next day or so when I called my fiancée, she began crying. I asked her what was wrong, and she told me she didn't want to lose me. I told her she was not going to lose me. I was scared I was going to lose her. She told me that I didn't understand. I waited a moment in silence, and that was when she told me that God was telling her to leave me. She was leaving me to go to a Christian university. I didn't want her to go because I was afraid she would get indoctrinated by a specific denomination of Christianity.

I was still very skeptical of the whole denomination issue with churches. I felt that if God is the same God, and they all read from the same Bible, there should not be all this division in the church that comes with the denominations. I still have trouble accepting the divisions but can see how it helps in identifying who is seriously following Christ. Serious followers of Christ exalt Jesus before a church denomination or the name of a church.

To make a long story short, my fiancée left me. I tried writing and calling her repeatedly, but my letters came back with a stamp from the post office saying, "Return to sender", and she would not accept the charges from my collect calls. I was heartbroken. I walked around outside wanting to just dive head first into the ground and hide under the dirt and grass and never come back up. But even during this super sorrowful time of my life, there was still that peace in my heart that only God can give a person. I had told my fiancée to just leave me when I first got locked up, but she said she would never leave me. People can't fulfill promises like that, for we don't know if we will even be alive tomorrow. But God can fulfill the promise of never leaving us. God was still with me, and his presence kept me alive when I felt so dead inside.

Chapter 50
"The Camp System"

The prison system in my state is basically split up into six levels. Levels ranged from a level 5, being the most secured, down to a level one, and then there was an unsecured level one that was the lowest of all the levels. Depending on how much time you have left to serve, and how good or bad behaved you are, determines what level you can go to. I started at a level 2 only because I had a minimum of 6 years to do. With good time, and the four months I had been credited for that I served in the county jail, the six years was only going to be 4 years and a few months. But then I found out about an early release program where I could get out even earlier. But the judge in my case, either contacted the early release program, or the prison itself and told them not to let me out early.

The prison I was at also had level 4 inmates at it, but they were usually separated from us. After doing two years at a level 2\4 facility, I was now eligible for the camp system. The camp system was considered an unsecured level 1 facility. Many of the inmates in a camp system went out into the free world and worked all day long on prison crews, and then came back to the prison basically to eat dinner and sleep. No one in the camp system had over three years left to serve in prison. They first sent me to what was the quarantine camp of the prison system. It was a shock to experience this place. I was used to being surrounded by guys doing life in prison and older people who had done a lot of time in prison already. The quarantine camp was filled with young kids who were not ever sentenced to much hard time and had not learned their lesson in life.

One night when I was about to ride out of this camp, I got sick and tired of some young black gangbanger kids that were keeping us up all night, so I told them to please be quiet. The main kid, along with four of his friends, came over and surrounded my bed. I was already planning in my mind how I would throw my blanket over one or two of them, smash the main kid in the face who was presently yelling in my ear only a foot away from me and then try to take out the other two before the last two got out from my blanket. I praised God when they all decided to back down and go to bed. This was the second time I was surrounded in prison by a small gang. The first time also ended well. It is never a good feeling though thinking you are about to be jumped by a group of people.

I couldn't wait to get out of this initial portion of the camp system. We lived in a barrack type of setting at this camp. I think there were probably 50 of us living in one room. I only spent a week or two at this camp, as did most inmates, because it was mainly a transition camp.

I was then sent way up north to the furthest northern portion of our state to a camp called Kitwin. It was in a town called Painsdale, and it was located in the thumb portion of our upper peninsula. Our state, the state of Michigan, consists of two peninsulas that resemble hands. Camp Kitwin was about a 7-hour drive from my town, a drive that my parents made every other week to visit me. This camp frightened me right away. The first night I was there I heard a guy getting beat up really bad with a padlock attached to a belt. I didn't know if I should leave our two-man cell or just stay out of it and mind my own business. I looked to my bunky and saw that he was not even fazed by the sounds of a guy screaming for his life. My bunky did not move, so neither did I.

I had started appealing my case on my own while at the level two prison. I had discovered that it was wrong for the judge to allow the bad evidence to be used in my trial. It was also wrong for the DA, in good faith, to use the bogus evidences. And the police did a shoddy job investigating my case. All of this resulted in me being unjustly sent to prison. I was waiting for the Michigan State of Appeals Court to answer the appeal I sent in to them.

The Appeals Court, as well as the State Supreme Court, denied my appeals. They gave me what people call a rubber stamp denial. It was a denial that just stated that I did not meet certain requirements. I thoroughly studied the requirements and had clearly met all of them. The State Appeals and Supreme Courts just didn't want to deal with my case. My hope was restored when I found out I could appeal to a higher level of courts called the Federal Courts, which had three levels to them. The Federal Court levels have greater authority than the state court levels do. I was hoping that the corruption only went as high as my state and that the Federal Courts would be more concerned about truth and justice. I needed access to a law library and informed the counselor at the camp that I was at of this need, and was transferred to a camp with a law library much closer to my hometown in a matter of just a few days.

I felt much better at the new camp I was transferred to. It was very laid back. Most of the inmates at this camp had their own individual cell with a key to it. I had to live in a 48-man barracks because I was there to use the law library and not there on a regular prison transfer but after a year of being there, they gave me my own cell. Getting my own cell was the best thing that happened to me in years. It was a taste of privacy that I wasn't used to. It felt awesome! The only fight I did get into while in prison was while I was in this 48-man barracks. A guy came at me and pulled me off of my top bunk bed. After hitting the floor, I immediately grabbed him by his throat, pinned him to a wall and tried to talk some sense into him. When I thought he was calmed down, I released him. Just as I was about to turn my back on him, he tried to punch me in my face. I deflected his fist, grabbed his throat, and pinned him to the wall again for a second conversation. I believe pinning him to the wall the second time saved him from great pain because his long hair was about to be sucked into the back of a massive floor fan. I thought I talked some sense into this man, but later he sent the biggest guy he could find to come and threaten me. Praise God though, this big guy was more sensible, and I did not have to pin him to a wall to reason with him. I am pretty sure I could not have pinned this guy by his throat to a wall. I most likely would have had to punch him in the face or throat before being able to restrain him on the ground.

Most of the prison guards at this camp remembered reading about me in the paper and thought it was horrible that they would throw me in prison for an accident. I had one person tell me that on millions of occasions, people drive drunk and that it was wrong that they punish the few who already suffer knowing they hurt or killed someone. Countless of people are all breaking the same law when they drive drunk, but the court system goes far harder after the ones who are the less fortunate. The guards thought it was even worse of a thing that the courts punished me for a crime someone else committed. For the most part, I had it good at this prison, as far as the guards went. If you were on the guard's bad side, it made prison far worse of a nightmare. The guards could write you tickets for petty things like giving a guy a ten cent dehydrated soup. A ticket usually resulted in top lock and loss of good time. Top lock meant they would take away your tv, and make you stay in your cell all day long for as many days as they decided. Loss of good time meant you had to spend more days in prison. A ten cent soup could cost you a lot, but other prison crimes could cost you a whole lot more.

Even though I had it good with most of the guards, there were a few guards that took a disliking to me. I had to go to prison court on a couple of different occasions. One was because a kitchen officer decided he was going to throw his weight around and tried to make me go outside and sit on the steps in the rain. I refused to do so, and he wrote me up for disobeying a direct order. Thank God a high ranking lieutenant had witnessed the entire event. I still had to go before a hearing investigator and be heard on the ticket. I was scared to plead not guilty at the hearing because I was told that if I pleaded guilty, I would probably just get lightly punished, but if I pleaded not guilty, the investigator would most likely side with the kitchen officer like he was known to do, and punished me much more severely for doing so, for telling the truth. I plead not guilty, and for what seemed like an eternity, the investigator sat there silently. He did, however, declare me not guilty and let me go with no punishment.

On my second time getting written a ticket, I was not so blessed. I had a prison officer who was my boss shove me around a little. He liked to play this way, but I did not find it funny. If I shoved him back and he told on me, I could be charged with an entirely new case and made to spend extra years in prison. So, I quit going to work and was ticketed for this. This time I didn't stand a chance before the hearings investigator. I tried to plead my case but wound up having to do two extra weeks in prison for this.

Overall though, this prison camp was like an oasis in my life's dark trial. I began to play beach volleyball with mostly other Christians. I bought a keyboard and began to learn how to play it. I also bought acrylic paints, brushes, and canvases and started to become a pretty good painter.

I joined a couple of prison bands and even started one of my own. I wrote at least four full stories and started a number of other ones that I wanted to publish once I was free from prison. I became heavily involved in the church at this camp. I helped organize holiday events, wrote skits, made songbooks, and even created some of my own songs. I stayed very busy while in prison. Staying busy helps time go by faster when you are locked up. It also helps you keep your mind off of the cold hard reality of being enslaved and kept away from all of your loved ones. I often felt like I was kidnapped and enslaved.

They make you work in prison. The first job the prison made me do was to be a referee. I was horrible at this job. I was never much of a sports fan, and things happened too fast for me to even see. Guys on the basketball court were punching each other right in front of me, but because I was trying to watch where the ball was, I often didn't even see the fist-to-face and other fowls being committed. The other referees hated anytime I even blew my whistle. They were big guys, and I was not. They often had to stand up for me when I made a call, even if they didn't agree with my call.

They wound up taking my whistle away and put me on the scoreboard. Even then, I often got yelled at because I didn't flip the numbers fast enough because I didn't know if it was a two or three-point basket that was made. And did I mention, I was the only white guy who was a basketball referee, and there were also no white guys on the basketball teams.

The four books I wrote while incarcerated are not really published yet per se. One I published titled "Pinky Pinkster" but regret not putting illustrations in it because it is more of a child's book. "Young Chastity" and "Three Storms from Heaven" have not made it through the editing process yet, and "The Christian Christmas Tree" I am going to redo and probably retitle it "The Greatest Christmas Tree". "Young Chastity" is more for teenagers. Three of these books are fictional but based on biblical scripture. "Three Storms from Heaven" is the one that is nonfictional. It is based on actual events I witnessed, events that have convinced me that God can control the weather.

Chapter 51
"The Appeals System"

The demand of working on my legal appeals also kept me very busy. Often, the courts would give you a very short time period to appeal your case to the next level and then they would take their sweet old time in making a decision. It was a *hurry up and wait* type of game. I never did get a good decision from any of the court levels. What I read in the law books made our judicial system look awesome! In theory, we have a great system. The whole appeals process is designed to be like a safety net to correct injustices that have occurred, and in my case, a great injustice had indeed occurred. The courts allowed the guy who killed three people to be rewarded a large amount of money, while at the same time, they put me in prison for a crime I did not commit.

What I discovered by reading the law books was that there were all types of reasons why they should overturn my case, or at the least, give me a new trial. Everything from how the judge allowed bad evidences to be used to falsely convict me, to how the DA did things that were not in "good faith", to how the police did a shoddy job in their investigations, even the fact that my attorney did not prove my innocence, all were good grounds for overturning my case or at the least, good grounds for giving me a new trial. The physical evidences that proved

Demon was the actual driver were also grounds to have my case overturned. The law books excited me. I read things about how the law was actually on my side. But what I found out through experience, is that the judges don't care about what case law says. I discovered that every safety net that there is, was rotted, and I fell through each and every one of them. I didn't just fall through some little cracks in the system, I fell through gaping holes.

Worse than discovering that our judicial system's safety nets are completely rotted out, is the fact that I also discovered that there are rules that are the opposite of safety nets. There are nets in exisistence that stop the truth from coming out, that stop justice from prevailing. The main one of these dark evil nets are time restrictions. If you don't get your appeal in by a certain time period, then it doesn't matter that you are unjustly incarcerated (in prison for a crime you did not commit). This blew my mind away. It takes countless of hours to figure out how to file an appeal and what level of court to file with, and what case law backs up your argument. It takes a long amount of time to teach yourself to be an attorney, and the prison only lets you go to the law library a few hours a day.

There are other safety nets that are supposed to protect you from this type of injustice. One of which I discovered was that at any time the trial judge sees that a person was wrongfully convicted in their courtroom, they can correct the injustice. When I discovered this I wrote Judge Heartless and asked him to correct the injustice done to me that happened in his courtroom. Heartless wrote me back telling me he could not help me. I showed him the information I found in the law books stating that he could (MCL 770.1). Then, Heartless wrote me back and told me he would not help me. It is one thing to tell someone you can't help them if you really can't; it is a completely different thing to tell them you won't help them when you can. He had the power to correct the injustice; he just would not do so.

As far as the bible is concerned, this shows that Heartless is not saved (going to heaven). It shows that he does not have the love of God in him. He was turning a deaf ear to my cries for justice. It is a fruit (sign) of a deeper issue. He could repent and get saved before he dies, but it would require a miracle and a great humbling on his part. I forgive him and have often prayed for him, but pride is what will probably prevent him from truly getting saved. As far as I know, he is a religious person, but religion does not get you into heaven. If anything, religion often prevents people from truly being saved (born-again). True Christianity is not a religion, it is a relationship, it is about being connected to God. The religion form of Christianity, just teaches you about God.

Chapter 52
"The Parole Board"

Shortly before going to the parole board I was informed that if I maintained my innocence, the parole board would most likely flop me (give me more time to do, deny me a parole). The parole board consists of three people who review your case and prison record, then decide if you should go free on parole. You are only interviewed by one of the three people, and the other two go off of this one person's report.

The lady I had to go to before looked evil. I know you cannot judge a book by its cover, but she certainly did not have an angelic appearance about her. She started off by reading out loud what was written about me in my file. She stated that I drove a car and crashed it into a tree and killed three people. She asked me if this was correct. I politely told her that it was not correct. She paused and silently re-read this portion of my file again. She then repeated what the file said out loud and said this is what it says, and this is what you were found guilty of. I then explained to her how it was not me who was driving the car.

The parole board member then told me that she had to put down that I was in denial and not accepting responsibility for a crime I committed. I tried my best to tell her that I was not in denial, that I was telling her the truth. I even told her that there was physical evidence that proved I was telling the truth. She didn't respond much and cut my interview short. From what I had heard, most interviews go much longer than mine did, and that because of the shortness of it, it was an indication that mine did not go well. Usually, they ask you questions about what you plan on doing once you are free to prevent you from committing the same crime. Since I was maintaining my innocence, she saw no need to talk about anything else; no need to talk about rehabilitation or a plan to prevent going back to prison, she had already made up her mind.

I waited for a month or so to hear back from the parole board. Most of the other inmates had already been told they got their paroles. I was told that I was probably going to get a one-year continuance or even a year and a half continuance. This meant they would add either a year or eighteen months to my sentence. Prisoners usually call getting a continuance, getting a flop. Just before I heard back from the parole board, I heard the Spirit tell me I was getting a 24-month continuance. I didn't want to believe it, but as it often happens, the Holy Spirit warns me of things, so I can better accept them when they happen. When the Spirit tells me things in advance, it also verifies to me that God sees what is happening to me, which brings me some comfort. Never-the-less, it was still extremely painful when I got the actual letter from the parole board stating that I had 2 more years added to my sentence. I felt like I was being punished for my faith, for doing what God tells us all to do, for being an honest man. And I was being more severely punished then others around me, for I had never heard of anyone else getting a 2 year flop while in the camp system.

So much for getting any of my good time. Because I was so well behaved in prison, I hadn't lost any of my good time up to this point. The two extra weeks I had to do in prison because of the ticket I got for not going to work, hadn't happened yet. The prison system had taken around fourteen months off my sentence for being well behaved. Now I was just given an additional 24 months for telling the truth. It is so backwards that our prison system would punish a man for telling the truth. I was warned that if I maintained my innocence, they would most likely punish me for it. As I had many times before, I prayed about whether I should just lie, but God himself kept telling me to tell the truth. Believe me, though I had joy in my heart even while I was locked up, I desperately wanted to get out of prison. But I was not so desperate that I was willing to lie about killing three people that I did not kill. God was and still is the source of my joy. As long as I keep obeying him, he keeps filling me with a joy rooted in heaven.

I still had appeals going on in the courts and was hoping that maybe one of the judges I appealed to would care enough about truth and justice, and make a just ruling in my behalf.

Chapter 53
"The Confession"

A lot took place during the extra two years I had to do in prison. I found out that my ex-fiancée fell off the deep end. From what I understand, she may have still been hoping to marry me. She was now in her fourth, and final year at the Christian university she was attending. She came home for Christmas break and found out I was given two more years to do. I only know bits and pieces about what happened to her, but it didn't sound good.

Here are the little pieces I heard. After Christmas break, she returned to the big city her school was in to finish up her last half a year there. The Muslim cab driver, who picked her up at the airport to take her back to school, somehow convinced her to move in with him. She got in trouble for living with someone she was not married to and got kicked out of the school. Christians are not supposed to marry Muslims and Muslims are not supposed to marry Christians.

A Muslim who genuinely follows their faith to the letter of the law, are actually supposed to kill Christians. A Christian who genuinely follows their faith, is supposed to love everybody and not follow the letter of the law. My ex-fiancée wound up marrying the Muslim guy. To this day, I wonder how she ever got this far off track. She used to walk so close to Jesus. I can only guess that she had returned to the city deeply saddened that I had to do two more years in prison, the cab driver told her she needed a drink to relax, she probably drank too much and wound up in his bed. After getting her kicked out of school, he probably felt bad for her and married her.

However it went down, it did not last long. He wound up telling her that she had to become Muslim or he could not stay married to her. She told him she could not do that, and he left her. I got a brief word from someone that they got back together for a very short time, but it still did not work out. Now they are divorced. I had hopes that maybe we would still get married, but later found out she married another guy. That marriage did not work out either.

The biggest thing that happened while I was serving the additional two years was Demon's confession. My brother ran into an old mutual friend of ours. I will call this friend "Priest". Priest asked my brother how I was doing in prison. My brother told Priest I was doing pretty good despite the fact that I was locked up for something I did not do. Priest told my brother he knew I was innocent. My brother asked Priest how he knew I was innocent. Priest said that while living out west in a different state with Demon, Demon came home one-night crying and said he had to get something off his chest. And that is when Demon told Priest he was the driver. It is as though Demon confessed his sins to a Priest, but a man named Priest, not a religious priest. My brother then informed my parents about what Priest told him. My parents came to visit me in prison that week and told me what my brother told them. I told them to tell my brother to tell Priest to go to the police. My parents told my brother what I said, but they also called the police and told them that Demon confessed to Priest. My parents and I were both very excited and thought this would now bring my innocence to light, and they would free me from prison. After all, the actual driver of the car confessed to the crime.

The police station was right across the street from where Priest worked. The police went to his work and asked him if Demon had confessed to him. He told the police that it was true. The police then asked Priest if he was willing to come to the station to be interviewed by them and to write out a written statement regarding the confession. The next day Priest went to the police station, did an interview with them, and signed a written statement.

My parents waited a little while hoping the court would automatically let me out now. They assumed that the police would tell the judge and DA and they would let me out and charge the guy who was the actual driver. When they hadn't gotten any word from the police or courts, they called and got a copy of the written statement.

I contacted the police station wondering what would happen now and asked if they were investigating the situation. They wrote me back saying that the DA told them not to investigate the case anymore, that the case was closed.

What? The courts and prosecutor just got word that a guy confessed to a crime and they just swept it under the rug. I couldn't believe it! I still gave heartless the benefit of the doubt. I thought that maybe he just couldn't see the truth for some reason, but now the truth was undeniable. I found out that the legal way I was supposed to proceed now was to start my entire appeals all over at the trial court level. I had already gone through the five higher courts with my appeals and had gotten no results. Now that I had newly discovered evidence that proved my innocence, I had a way to start my appeals all over. I first had to go to the judge who tried me and sent me away unjustly. I thought for sure he would do the right thing now. How could a person not? But he did not.

Heartless ruled that Priest was not a reliable witness because he got the year of the confession wrong. Priest had stated that Demon confessed ten years prior, that it was after Demon got the money from the car accident, but Demon only got the money eight years prior. This was pathetic. Priest was trying to remember back eight to ten years and got the time a little messed up. What year the confession happened wasn't what was so important. What was far more important was the fact that the confession happened. The judge was throwing the baby out with the bathwater. The judge just looked for any stupid excuse he could to not overturn my case.

Heartless ruled that Priest was not a reliable witness because he had a hard time remembering whether the confession happened 8 or ten years prior, yet Demon changed his story 4 times to the police about who was driving the car during the accident. The year the confession happened was a minor issue. Demon changing his story to the police was a major issue, a much more major issue. Heartless just proved without a doubt that he was a terrible, heartless, and unjust judge.

From what I heard, he is a man who goes to church every Sunday. It goes to prove that some churches are not doing a good job teaching people right from wrong. Some church leaders do not have the Spirit of God in them. They can't teach people how to receive the Spirit of God into their lives if they themselves don't have God's Spirit within them. It is the blind leading the blind. Those who wanted Jesus crucified were the religious leaders of his day. What really blows my mind is that many non-church goers are not nearly as heartless as Heartless. He gives his church a bad name.

Chapter 54
"The Parole Board Again"(Joseph)

I had to go to the parole board a second time after I finished doing the additional 2 years they gave me the first time I went before them. When I went before the one board member this second time, I took a copy of Priest's statement of Demon's confession. I also took a copy of the pages of my trial and police report that showed there was physical evidence that also proved Demon was the driver.

The parole board member didn't even look at the papers I brought him. He slid them back across the table to me and said that he did not care about it. He then told me that as long as I maintained my innocence, the parole board would not ever let me go. He basically told me I would have to do six more years if I kept telling the truth. I had already done six long years, and I did not look forward to doing six more, but God did not want me to lie about being the driver.

I told the parole board member that I had read an article in a paper about how a parole board in another state exonerated an innocent man. He told me he was not going to exonerate me. The strangest thing about my meeting with this parole board member was that he had my name written down as Joseph. My name is Jash. I have had a lot of people call me Josh, Jason, Jack, Jase, Jay and even a few other close similar names, but I had never had anyone call me Joseph on accident before. I found this as a sign from God, again confirming he knew what I was going through and that he was with me. Joseph was a man in the Old Testament who went through a hard time in life and wound up getting thrown into prison for a crime he did not commit also. Joseph was 17 when he was sold into slavery, then falsely thrown into prison, and he was not freed until over 12 years later. I was 17 when they charged me and enslaved me with bond stipulations, and now they were telling me I was going to spend over 12 years in prison for something I did not do. I believe being called Joseph, the age I was when accused falsely, and having to do so many years in prison unjustly, were too similar to just be a coincidence.

I still pursued my appeals and took the newly discovered evidence to each level of the court system. If nothing else, I felt God wanted me to be a witness against the evils of the judicial system's judges. They will all be without excuse on the Day of Judgment. Jesus tells us in the book of Matthew chapter 25 in the New Testament that whatever we do to those in need around us, is how we are treating Jesus, and that we will be judged by what we do or don't do for others in need. I needed a judge to be concerned about truth and justice. Nothing goes unnoticed by God. I did get to see one of the judges I appealed to after I was freed. She was very decrepit looking. She was skin and bones and very worn out looking. Her voice was horrible to listen to. She looked like she had one foot in the grave. I delivered a bed to her house. She pointed a bony finger at her heated blanket and said, "It is over there" in a type of voice that sounded like a wicked witch. Two weeks later she was dead. But her spirit still exists. I do not think she is in heaven though. Maybe I am wrong. Maybe she got born again before passing on. I doubt it though. The older a person is, the less likely they are to get born again. Many people make their decision at an early age. They either decide to pursue God, or follow the ways of the world. No decision; is still a decision. It is a decision to not do anything. If you say "No, I am not going to make a decision to follow God today", you still made a decision.

God is just. People say they believe in karma. Call it what you want, the Bible says you will reap what you sow. If you sow to the sinful nature, you will reap death. If you sow to the Spirit, you will reap life. If you do wrong, wrong will happen to you. If you do good, good will come to you. Sometimes good things do happen to bad people, and bad things happen to good people, but usually, this is a result of other people disobeying God.

Chapter 55
"Tree and Broken Knees"

Do you remember me talking briefly about a woman I called "Tree"? She was the one who interviewed me for rehab and told me she was going to lie to the judge and tell him I had a drinking problem even though she told me she did not believe I did. I later read the report she sent to the judge. The report was horrible. She made me look like a crazy guy who was hearing voices in my head. I couldn't believe she did what she did. She told me she was going to lie to the judge, but in actuality, I think she lied to me.

I remember there being a really bad wind storm one day. The prison camp I was presently incarcerated at was on the edge of a state forest, and I remember hearing all sorts of tree breaking in the woods because of this strong wind. A few days later I saw Tree's obituary in the paper. The obituary didn't say how she died though. I told my parents it was strange that she died so young.

My parents told me that she was driving down the street during that big wind storm and that there was a tree branch laying on the road. She got out of her car to move the branch, and the wind blew the rest of the tree down on her. I talked to a fellow inmate in the prison yard who was sad when he heard about Tree's death. He told me she was a good Christian woman. I told him that was not what I experienced with her. Even Hitler was thought to be a good person by some people. I am sure even the worst of people alive today are viewed as good people to someone. Hitler's mom may have been given everything she needed and heart desired, including fine golden jewelry from her boy. She may have spoken highly of him and saw him as good. Judge Heartless may appear to be a saint to some people. What matters is how God sees us. There is always someone to fool, but no one can pull the wool over God's eyes.

One guy, who I will call "Hammer", was getting out of prison soon. He said he was going to my town when he got out and asked me if I wanted him to break Demon's legs. He told me it was wrong what Demon did to me and said he knew a way he could break both his kneecaps with a ball-peen hammer to where Demon would never walk again. I told the guy that I did not want him to break Demon's legs. Say I had told Hammer to break Demon's legs, and say he got caught and then said it was my idea. We would have gotten new prison sentences to do. But it was not the fear of being kept in prison that made me not want to take revenge on Demon. It was my love and fear of God. If God wanted Demon to never walk again, he could do it, and no one could charge God with a crime. We are told in the Bible not to take vengeance, but to leave room for God's wrath.

Chapter 56
"Karma vs. The Wrath of God"

Let's talk about Karma. It is defined as; your actions affect your future, good deeds bring you future happiness, while bad deeds bring you future suffering. I see God's wrath as far greater than just good or bad feelings or a futuristic payback or reward. Karma is more of a godless society's way of explaining God's wrath, it is a sugar coating of the harsher reality that exists.

The fear is not as great if you suffer and just chalk it up as something you deserved, and you have now reaped the full punishment. It is a much greater fear to believe you are under the wrath of God, and this wrath will not stop until you either repent or wind up in hell. The wrath of God can save a person's soul if they allow it to draw them near to God, to accept his grace and mercy, and to repent of their wrongdoings.

I got the news one day while in prison that Demon fell out of a canoe and broke his neck. I was told that he was now a quadriplegic. Was this the wrath of God? You tell me? The guy crashed my car, almost killed me, did kill three kids, took thirty some thousand dollars that was supposed to go to the families of the three kids, and lied and sent me to prison for 12 years! The Bible makes it clear that God is just, and that vengeance is his, and that he repays wrongdoings. I would say yes, Demon breaking his neck did involve God. One can accuse God of being cruel, for breaking his neck, or allowing it to happen, but a wise man can see the grace of God in it. Demon now has time to repent and get right with God and spend an eternity in heaven. God could have allowed him to drown when he broke his neck, and he would most likely have wound up in hell. Life on earth is but a breath compared to eternity. It is far better to lose a body part like a hand or eye, even the use of all four limbs and wind up in a wonderful place too great to describe with words, then to stay completely whole and wind up in a horrible, terrifying place for all of eternity.

When I first got word about Demon, I fell to my knees, cried and began to pray. Part of me was glad to see God's vengeance, but a bigger part of me felt so bad for Demon. I always saw being paralyzed as the worst thing that could happen to a person. I have heard people tell me to just kill them if they ever become paralyzed. Being paralyzed is a form of prison that there is no paroling from. I cried out to Jesus and said, "I have heard that you experienced all types of the bad things that we do in life when you came and lived on this earth; but when did you ever experience being a quadriplegic?" It took me a moment, but then I saw Jesus hanging on the cross in my spirit, and it dawned on me; that while he was nailed to the cross, he was a quadriplegic. Jesus didn't say a word to me. He just let me see a vision of him hanging on the cross. I could see that during his experience of being nailed to the cross, he could not use his arms or legs.

God is merciful! Anyone who is alive still has a chance to be saved and go to heaven. Heartless, Demon, even the DA can truly accept Jesus Christ as their Lord and Savior and go to heaven. The Bible says that the way to eternal life is narrow and only a few will find it. There are many other people out there just like heartless who won't ever accept the truth though.

My job is to just tell the truth, and whether people accept it or not, that is up to them. Have you ever heard the saying, "you can take a horse to water, but you can't make it drink the water"? But I believe that you can make a horse want to drink water by giving it something salty to eat. I am the salt. My testimony is salt. Hopefully, some of you are thirsty for Jesus by now. If so, ask him right now to save you. If you skipped chapter 40 earlier, it might be time to go back and read it now. If not, hopefully someday in your near future you will be ready to get saved.

Chapter 57
"The Parole Board Once Again"

Even though my last time at the parole board was very bad and the parole board member said I was not going to get out until I maxed out in six more years, I still had to keep going before the parole board. The most they could give me was a single 24-month continuance at a time, but for some reason, they were only giving me 18 months at a time. So, after another 18 months, I had to go before the parole board for the third time. Before my hearing date, my prison counselor called me to his office and told me I had to lie and say I was the driver. I told him that God did not want me to lie. I also told him that the Bible says all liars are going to be thrown into the lake of fire. My counselor told me that a lot of people must be going to hell then. I told him that is also something the Bible says is true, that the path to eternal life is narrow and few people take this path, but the path to destruction is wide, and many people take that path. (Matthew 7:13-14).

My prison counselor then got mad at me and said that he would be under the desk he was sitting at giving him sexual favors to get out of prison. I was disgusted at even the thought of what he said. I told him that I am not him and that I would not ever do anything like that. He basically got angrier and told me to get out of his office after that, which I was glad to do so.

This time my parole board hearing was supposed to be done remotely through a television monitor. Since our prison did not have the proper equipment to do this, they took us to a different prison to hold our parole hearings. It just so happened to be, that this other prison was in my home county that I had not seen in over eight years. The funny thing was, the parole board member was there in person. So there really was no need to drive nearly a hundred inmates an hour away when just the one parole board member could have drove to our prison. I now wonder if the whole thing was set up just to get me to see my old county as an attempt to get me to lie. Maybe they thought if they made me homesick enough I would cave in and disobey God.

This parole board meeting was no different than the first two. I told them the truth and hoped that maybe this member was less heartless than the last two, but this was not the case. I received another 18-month continuance. This was my third continuance. I got a 24-month one the first time, and now two 18-month continuances. I originally came up for parole a little over four years after getting locked up. Now I had received an additional 5 years.

Around this time, I read a scripture in the Bible I had never remembered seeing before. It rang a bell in my soul because of how the words sounded so much like what Demon's mother had written to me. It said, "…she who said to me, 'Where is the LORD your God?' My eyes will see her downfall;…" Just prior to this verse the scripture said, "Do not gloat over me, my enemy! Though I have fallen, I will rise. Though I sit in darkness, the LORD will be my light." It sure felt like Demon's mother was gloating over me when she asked me, "where is your God at now?" when I had first gotten locked up. And now, I felt I was seeing her downfall. Her son is now injured for life, and I have heard she is the one who has to bath him and wipe his butt every day.

Even now, I feel bad for Demon. He was only seventeen years old when the accident happened. He did not purposely kill the three children; that was an accident. But his lying about it, and sending me to prison for it; that was not by accident, but was a conscious decision, that was done purposely. Even so, I forgive him. I sometimes even make excuses for him.

After all, he had the police on his back wanting him to tell them who was driving, and he feared going to prison. He must feel horrible for accidentally killing his best friend and their two girlfriends. I am sure he also feels bad about sending me to prison. I can only imagine how the DA had repeatedly questioned him about the accident and probably threatened to charge him with all sorts of crimes if he changed his story and came clean. He could have been charged with all sorts of crimes, and possibly still can be. Most crimes have a statute of limitations, meaning you can't be charged with them so many years after you committed them. But I have heard that when there is a death involved, there is no statute of limitations. He could have been charged with lying to police officers, for committing perjury on the stand, with insurance fraud, and with the deaths of the three children. He has committed numerous crimes, but the DA has never even tried to go after him for one of these crimes. To do so, would mean that the DA would have to admit he made a mistake and sent me to prison unjustly.

The saddest thing about the legal aspect of what happened, is that if Demon had confessed right away to what he did, and showed a little remorse for killing his best friend; he probably would have done 6 months in the county jail and maybe a year or two of probation. Instead, I did nearly four long hard years on bond and over 12 years hard time in prison. Having three felonies on my record also makes it hard to get a decent job, let alone any job. I also had to fight to get my driver's license back. I had to walk everywhere when I first got released from prison. At this point of the story, I was still in prison though. Let me talk a little more about what I experienced while on the inside.

Chapter 58
"Vision of Jesus"

While in prison I often liked to get other prisoners to turn their hearts and minds toward God. One way I was doing this was by walking around outside on the prison yard's track asking inmates if they knew what was coming up soon? Easter was quickly approaching, and I used this as an opportunity to witness to the convicts. I would ask them if they knew what holiday was almost here, if they didn't know, I would tell them. Then I would ask if they knew what was celebrated on Easter. This always opened a door for me to tell them about how Jesus died and then rose again to take away our sin and to save us from going to hell.

On Good Friday, I talked to numerous guys in prison and told them that today was the day Jesus died on the cross and explained to them why he had to die. Then on Easter Sunday I did the same thing and told other guys that today was the day Jesus rose from the dead. But once Easter had come and gone, I still wanted to ask guys the question if they knew what Jesus did today. I wasn't sure what Jesus was doing today since it was now after Easter. I tried to imagine that he was in heaven building a house for each of us. After all, he told his disciples (and us) that in heaven there is many mansions and that he was going to prepare a place for them (and us). But it was hard to imagine Jesus wearing a tool belt with pure sterling silver nails in it while banging together some golden two by fours.

Then one of the most amazing things happened to me when I was at a Monday night Bible study/church service. During praise and worship, I suddenly saw a vision. I saw the side and back of Jesus. I was standing a little off to his side and sort of behind him. He was standing there with royal clothes on. I noticed that in front of him were thousands and thousands of beings praising him. I wasn't sure if the beings were angels or people. I wanted so badly to be in that crowd praising him. I didn't know why I was standing up next to him. Later it dawned on me that the Bible says, we, the body and bride of Christ, are seated with him in the heavenly realms.

I cried a little when I experienced this heavenly realm vision. I now new exactly where Christ was. He is not walking around heaven with a tool belt on and hammer in hand. He is sitting on his throne in glory being praised by all of heaven, and we his bride, are sitting by his side.

Chapter 59
"Still on the Inside"

When you are in prison, on the inside of the barbed wire fences and bars, you call it just that, "being on the inside". You refer to the people, or your old life, as being on "the outside", or "In the world". When I was in the world, I never knew much about the inside.

Once on the inside, my heart broke time and time again for the people in there. I liken being locked up as a sort of death. You are cut off from most of the people you once knew. Many people on the inside have very little contact with the outside; especially the poorer inmates whose family can't afford to drive hundreds of miles to visit them or pay the overpriced collect call fees in order to accept the inmates' calls. Many inmates can barely afford stamps, paper, and pens to even write their loved ones.

Most inmates are hungry for love. Usually, I did not even know how much I was touching people in prison. One day, a man who was locked in the cell next to mine, was about to be released from prison. He handed me a beautiful fleece lined flannel shirt. It was blue and white and looked brand new. It was really the only possession he was taking home. He said he saved it so that he had something nice to wear once he was free, but he handed it to me and thanked me for being so nice to him. Again, I felt the electric shock in my soul from God when he handed me the fleece flannel jacket. I was surprised at how touched most inmates were by the smallest acts of kindnesses I showed them.

Don't get me wrong, there are still very wicked prisoners in prison, but I met a lot of decent people on the inside. I am still friends with some of them. Many people in prison are decent people who just made a poor decision or two. One bad moment in your life can lead to many years in prison or even life in prison. I had one bunky in prison who was doing life for killing his wife. I heard that killing her was a complete accident, but then he freaked out and tried to hide her body by sending her through a wood chipper. This bunky of mine had been locked up for over thirty years when we became bunkies. I am certain that he would not hurt anyone in society if ever freed, but one mistake in life can cost you life in prison.

Other guys I had met who had been locked up for long periods of time got caught up in the gang life when they were young but were now much older and wiser, and if ever given a chance to be free, they would be a blessing to society, not a threat to it. These types of people are considered God's treasures. Just as mankind keeps his treasures locked up and secure, so does our Father God. Many of God's treasures are locked up in prison. I have seen talented people on the inside who have skills that far exceeds many professionals in the free world. I saw a guy who could throw a football more accurate and further than probably any NFL quarterback. I saw basketball players that if they had the same breaks as some of the NBA players had, they would have been right up there with the best. I also met singers, rappers, artists and more. And there are truly humble and good-hearted people in the inside. It is too bad we don't make better avenues at freeing some of these people. You could probably release half of our state's prisoners today and not hurt our society, but rather help it. It costs a lot to keep people locked up.

When I was locked up, I heard it cost over $50,000 a year to keep me locked up. That means it cost the taxpayers over $600,000 to keep me locked up for over 12 years. I was seventeen years old when the accident happened. I was seventeen years old when Demon crashed my car. Is a seventeen-year-old who had an accident such a threat to society that we should pay $600,000 to keep them locked up?

In my particular case, they were making taxpayers pay over a half a million dollars because of my honesty. But in so many cases, we are paying large amounts of money to keep people locked up that really should not be in there. In my mind, The DA, judge, some of the police officers involved in my case, even Demon's mother are far more wicked people who are more damaging to our society than the people behind bars. In many cases, we are locking up the wrong people. Maybe it would be wise to make DA's and judges do a month in prison before they can even take the jobs they do where they are involved in locking people up, so that they realize and experience firsthand what they are doing to people.

Maybe they would not be so quick to fill up our prisons then, and quit spending so many of our taxpayer dollars keeping so many people locked up for so long. I know of one particular case in my town where the judge sentenced an 18-year-old to over three times the amount of time recommended under our state's guidelines.

Chapter 60
"I Like Prison"

I often got made fun of because of how much I smiled while I was locked up. I knew it was because I had God in my heart and because I could still serve my God even though I was behind bars. Many people this day and age have idols in their lives, they are serving false gods. A thing that can be a false god is a drug or sex addiction. While locked up, many people cannot serve these false gods. Some find ways to get the drugs or turn to homosexuality, but most of the inmates who don't serve the OTG (One True God), are miserable because they can't do what they were doing. It goes even deeper than just addictions. Many people are slaves to sin and can't be good slaves while locked up. They serve their own evil desires or even Satan himself but don't realize it.

I was able to serve (obey, follow, walk beside) Jesus even while incarcerated. This gave me joy indescribable in my soul. I smiled a lot while locked up. One day when we had to get new identification cards made, I was in a waiting room with over fifty other inmates. When it was my turn to get my picture taken I smiled. This was always my tradition when getting my photo taken. All of the inmates got strangely quiet when I sat in the chair that the photographer made us sit in. As soon as I smiled, everyone bust out laughing. I heard one guy yell out, "I told you he would smile". Even the photographers often couldn't believe I was smiling for my prison id card. Most inmates wanted to look as mean and angry as they could for their mug shot. Sometimes the photographer would make me hold my smile for an extra period of time because they were confused.

Often when a prison guard asked for my id and saw me smiling on it, they would say something along the lines that "you must love prison". I would also hear inmates yell out or whisper "I love prison" when I walked by them. One officer even brought up my picture on a computer and showed me that I was smiling on the prison website. I told him that the picture he was showing me was the same picture that was on my id card. One younger black guy stopped me on the way to the chow hall one day and asked me why I was smiling so much. I told him it was because of Jesus and he told his friends that were sitting with him that he had told them so. My reason for smiling must have been their reason for debate.

When I had first got to prison, a guy who had seen me walking the track said he saw me smiling, and he assumed that I was gay. Many gay guys in prison smile a lot because they are very happy to be surrounded by nothing but big strong men. When the guy who saw me smiling found out I was not gay, he said he wanted what I had. He gave this testimony while at one of the church services. Everyone laughed when he told them about what he first thought of me, but then rejoiced when he said he discovered what I had at these services. I can't take credit for what this man saw, wanted, and then found. He saw Jesus in me, wanted Jesus in his life, and then accepted him into his life.

I had to take a number of drug tests while in prison. I never thought very much about why I had to take so many drug tests. I knew that they seemed to drug test people who got a lot of visits because most drugs were smuggled in through the visiting room. But one day, while I was out walking in the prison yard, a prison guard said I was too happy for being in prison. He told me he was going to have me drug tested. It was not a normal protocol to tell an inmate that you were going to have them drug tested. Guards were not supposed to say a whole lot to inmates regarding things like this.

But it opened my eyes as to why I probably had to take so many drug tests. I was called in for a drug test a day after the guard had said something to me. I tried to quit smiling so much after that, but it was too difficult for me. I had already been down over ten years by this time, what were a few more years of drug tests anyway? So, I went back to my good old smiling self. Don't get me wrong, I did shed countless of tears while locked up, but even then, God gave me joy in the midst of my sorrow, and I would say I smiled more than I cried.

I think many guys in prison purposely make their faces look mean as a way to keep predators away from them. I did draw a certain amount of predators and bugs, but God protected me the entire time I was locked up. A predator usually wants to harm you or worse, and a bug is what they call an annoying guy who bugs you a lot, usually by begging you for stuff like commissary food, coffee or cigarettes on a regular basis.

Chapter 61
"Prison Transfer"

After spending nearly 7 years at the prison close to my town I was transferred to another prison down by the bottom of our state. This prison was located in a town called Coldwater. It was in the center of the wrist of our hand looking state. The city I was from is located in the pinky pit of the hand, where a wedding ring would touch the pinky at. It was nice to have a change, but there were also many things not so nice about this new prison. It was a bigger prison, so there were many more inmates at it. This prison started a dog program where they took in greyhound dogs that could no longer race. Most of these dogs were still very young. Inmates would train these dogs to be good pets and then the dogs would be sold. It was a very interesting program.

Coldwater had Christian services completely run by inmates. It wasn't long before I became a church board member. I played a keyboard and was eventually put in charge of praise and worship. As time went on and members of the board either went home or got transferred, I was moved up to the assistant pastor position. The time came when they wanted to make me the pastor of this church of around 80 inmates. I turned down the position mainly because it put a target on you and was a lot of responsibility. I didn't mind preaching once in a while and helping, however I could, but I didn't need to be the main target in this prison. Non-Christians loved to try and point out the flaws of our inmate pastor and try to even get him to fight or do other wrong things. Even other Christians often targeted whoever was the main pastor, as did prison guards. I preferred to do whatever I could to assist our pastors but didn't want to be the pastor myself.

Besides leading worship, I made songbooks for our church services at Coldwater, put together holiday events and wrote a play while there. I also wrote a book and learned how to paint better while at this prison far from home. I kept very busy as usual. I didn't have any legal work to do since I was just waiting for the next court level to decide if they were going to follow suit with the other unjust judges or if they were going to see to it that justice prevailed. I was close to the highest court I could possibly appeal to in our country. My legal argument at this time was that newly discovered evidence had come forth proving my innocence. But it wasn't that simple. The courts kept saying that I did not appeal to them quick enough, that under the anti-terrorism death penalty act, I only had one year to appeal. I argued that this act/law was not designed to keep an innocent man in prison.

I can't believe that there are laws that stop an innocent man from being released from prison. I also can't believe that our parole board has policies that prevent them from releasing an innocent man that was unjustly convicted. They just kept telling me that as long as I kept telling the truth, they would not let me go. It is not right to punish a man for being honest. I had hopes that maybe things would be different at Coldwater, but my hopes were dashed to the ground when I had to see the parole board again. They showed no mercy but instead gave me one more 18-month continuance. To add to the bad news, I was denied my next appeal as well.

Even though these two things happened repeatedly to me in prison, I never fully got used to them. I always kept thinking I was going to be freed any day in the near future. I kept hoping that either a truly just judge would get my case, or a parole board member would be concerned about the truth and let me out. Every time my hopes got crushed it stung me for a few days in my soul. I would often walk around numb and have to call on Jesus extra hard to restore my joy again. I came to accept and realize that in this world we will suffer, and that the life after this one is far more important. Since I was denied my latest appeal, I needed a law library so that I could appeal once again to the next higher court level. I told my prison counselor and was quickly transferred back to Camp Lehman in Grayling Michigan, the closest prison I could go to near my hometown.

Chapter 62
"Back to Camp Lehman"

Just before I had left Camp Lehman the first time, they had decided to double up the one-man cells. The good thing about my returning to the camp was that they did not make me stay in a 48 man barracks this time around. I was put right into a two-man cell. My newest bunky was a devout Jew. A young man who locked across the hall and down a few cells, was soon to become one of my best friends. He had a strong will and hot fire in his soul to follow Jesus. He also had a mother who lived in my hometown that happened to have the same first name as my mother and very similar middle name. I will call this man Strong Will. Another two good friends still in my life I had met the first time I lived at this prison. I will call them Rich and Apple.

When Apple was released from Camp Lehman, he had gone to my hometown to try and talk Demon into coming clean so that I could get out of prison. My parents had hired a detective around this same time to try and talk to Demon as well. This happened after Priest had come forth and talked to the police about how he had heard Demon confess to the crime. Demon would not meet with my friend Apple because he was convinced that Apple was a detective that had been looking for him. I was very thankful and blessed to have a friend like Apple who was willing to travel such a long distance to try and help me. His heart was right with Christ as well. He was not the guy who asked me if I wanted him to go break Demon's knees.

Strong Will, on the other hand, was not eligible for parole until after my max out date. I was now one year from my max out date. The way a man's prison sentence works is that he is given an earliest release date and a max out date. If a man is good in prison, he is usually let out on his earliest release date. I was as good as a man could be in prison. Even though I had come very close to getting into a few fights, I only ever threw one guy up against a wall and held him there until he came to his senses. I took any and every class they made me take. I earned all of my good time days, which made my earliest out date even earlier. I was only ever found guilty of one ticket while locked up, yet despite all of this, I was told I was going to be maxed out, and that I would do over eight extra years in prison past my minimum out date.

The entire reason the parole board gave for doing this, was my continual honesty, or as they called it, my denial of the truth, my maintaining of my innocence. You would think, that after they made me do 2 or 3 extra years in prison, that maybe I wasn't actually in denial. Why make a guy do 8 extra years for telling the truth? One day I was informed that I was up for seeing the parole board one last time. By this time, I only had one year left till my max out date. Even if they gave me a parole this time, I would still have to finish my max out date on parole. I didn't see the point in even going to the parole board, so I signed off on my right for a hearing. I was told that if I did not go to the hearing they could not give me a parole. It made no difference to me at this point. I was denied my last and final appeal as well with the court system. I just looked at the entire prison and judicial system as a joke. Neither of them cared about truth, justice or truly rehabilitating a person. I also saw it all as a big test of my faith. I still trusted that God was good and I desired to follow him even though it cost me dearly. Mankind is the one that evil resides in. God is holy. I would rather obey God and suffer the wrath of mankind than obey mankind and suffer the wrath of God. The Bible even warns us not to fear those (mankind) who can kill the body, but rather fear the One (God) who can kill the body and then throw your soul into hell.

Chapter 63
"Maxed Out"

My max out day finally came, and I was spit out of the belly of the beast (I was set free from prison). After over 12 long years, I was a free man. I had no parole with burdensome stipulations like people get when they get a parole. I had completely served and maxed out a sentence for a crime I did not commit. I felt like the world tried all that it could to get me to sell my soul, but the world was unsuccessful. It didn't stop there though. Now that I was free I couldn't wait to get back to my hometown and do all that I could to evangelize the world. I had a few short stories that I had written while locked up that I couldn't wait to publish. I also had drawn some scrolls that I wanted to produce for children that explained biblical truths.

I moved back in with my parents. They had built a new beautiful house right on the edge of our city. The very day I got out of prison I went to a print shop to make copies of my scrolls.

Easter was just around the corner, and I wanted to get my Easter scroll out on the market for people to purchase. I figured that the Easter scroll I had designed was a great Easter Basket accessory. I made some up as quick as I could and took them to a local Christian store where they put them on the first main display that you saw when you walked through their front entrance. I sold enough to encourage me to make more the following year.

My biggest two shocks coming out of prison were cell phones and the price of everything. When I first got locked up gas was under one dollar a gallon, now it was nearly four dollars. The price of everything was ridiculous to me. It seemed that the cost of everything skyrocketed, yet minimum wage had not done the same. It didn't matter much because I couldn't even find a minimum wage job. Most businesses around my parents' house wanted people to apply online for a job. On paper, I looked horrible! I had three felonies and no work history or job references in over 12 years. I painted a picture and put it for sale online, and it sold very quickly. Though everything cost a lot, it was hard for me to sell anything for a similarly high price.

I couldn't find anyone local to print one of my books at a reasonable price. I wanted to keep the price low on my Christmas story "The Christian Christmas Tree" (Soon to be retitled "The Greatest Christmas Tree"). Most print places wanted more money to print my book than I even wanted to sell it for. I did find one print shop that could print my book, but they could not bind it. So I bought colored duct tape and hand bound my books. I planned on selling my book at craft shows and local bookstores. I found three stores willing to sell my book.

One was the Christian store that I sold my scrolls at. They let me do a book signing at their downtown store. At each of the craft shows, I was signing the books for everyone as well.

I liked this book writing business and wondered if I could possibly make a career out of it. I then borrowed nearly a thousand dollars from a man I had just met that day at a church. I told him I just needed a one-month loan and used the money to run an ad in a worldwide Christian magazine. I think I only sold one book from the ad, and my sales at the craft shows by this time were not doing any good. Came to find out, the local craft shows have a lot of the same people who attend each show. You can only sell so many books to the same group of people. I needed to go to craft shows out of my town if I wanted to keep selling books, but I was not allowed to drive. I did however sell around 700 copies of my book locally.

I had gone to the secretary of state to inquire about getting my driver's license back and was told I just had to bring in a certain amount of identification and pay a small fee and I could get my license. When I returned to the secretary of state around a month later, they now told me I had to contact their main headquarters, because I couldn't get my license until I did everything the headquarters required. Come to find out, they were requiring a lot from me. I had to take three different driving tests over a one-year period, had to have a breathalyzer ignition switch added to my vehicle, go in for an alcohol drug evaluation, take a drug test and more. I was given a restricted driver's license for the year I had a breathalyzer in my minivan that I had to blow through to start and then blow through periodically to keep it running. I was only allowed to drive from home to work. I did get a job at a local business unloading delivery trucks. It took me 8 months to land a job. A guy took pity on me and offered me 5 hours a week unloading trucks. I was also self-employed as an author and scroll artist. I did put my scrolls all over town at small mom and pop businesses. I made a small Easter basket display with an attached container for donations.

When my year with the breathalyzer was up, I had to go downstate to be interviewed by a head honcho with the secretary of state in order to get my driver's license fully reinstated. This interview was done via a television screen. I couldn't figure out why they make a guy who does not have a driver's license go over an hour's drive away to have an interview through a television screen when there was a much larger secretary of state right in my hometown.

I feel like they just try to make things as complicated as they can to discourage people from going through the entire process and that the government agencies are messed up and inefficient. I did everything they required, but I received a letter in the mail saying my driver's license was denied because I did not meet all of the requirements but didn't tell me what requirement I didn't meet. This was so déjà vu to me. This was the same type of excuse that the courts gave me repeatedly through my years and years of appeals to them. I went through all of my paperwork and didn't see anything I missed doing. I appealed the secretary of state's decision and sent them the proofs of everything I did. After waiting what seemed like an eternity, I received a letter stating I could now get my driver's license back.

It was a wonderful freedom feeling to get my driver's license back. Now I presently drive a delivery truck full-time for a living and was also driving for Uber. Who would have thought that a guy with three felonies and a super blackened driver's record would wind up with a job where he drives a big truck every day? It is so like God to do things like this. I go into people's homes to deliver them new beds, sometimes when no one is even home. Usually, guys with felonies can't get any sort of job that allows them to go into people's homes. Most businesses won't even give me an opportunity to prove myself operating a cash register, and now I have a boss who has told me he wants to sell me his business in five years. I thank God that there are people out there who are not controlled by fear and who were willing to give me the breaks I needed; people who don't judge a book by its cover.

Chapter 64
"Falling Back in Love"

A year after I was freed from prison, I went to a church to see if they were interested in buying some of my Easter scrolls. While at this church, I noticed a sign stating that they were having a singles group meeting that night. I asked if I could attend and they told me I could.

That night I met the woman I knew I was going to marry. We stayed later than anyone else at this group and still didn't want to leave when they were cleaning up the place. I was helping out at a church once a week with its youth group and went there that night after meeting this beautiful woman. My friend from prison, who I call Strong Will, was there that night. Strong Will agreed with me that I truly met the woman I was going to marry. He asked if he could be my best man, and exactly three months to the day we met, me and Trisha were married.

We give God the glory for our marriage. It is not normal for people to marry after only knowing each other for a few months. We were planning our wedding within the first month of meeting one other. We completely saw God's hand in our midst and thanked him repeatedly for each other. I did have doubts at times and questioned if another woman I had briefly dated was the one I was supposed to marry, but I don't believe that God makes us marry a certain person. I had a chance to marry either the one woman I had dated briefly or this new woman I was presently dating. God gives us a choice, he does know what and who is best for us, but when it comes down to it, the choice is ours, and I believe I chose the one who was best for me. Once the choice is made though, God wants us to be faithful to the one we marry and to commit ourselves to that person. The Bible says that God hates divorce. I can see why God hates divorce. Divorce makes things difficult for people, especially when there are children involved. Divorce, however, is not the one unforgivable sin that the Bible talks about. The only unforgivable sin that there is, is blasphemy of the Holy Spirit.

You basically get out of marriage what you put into it. I discovered that it does require a lot of sacrifice on your part to be married to another, and it requires even more of a sacrifice once you have children. And that is exactly what came next in my life. My wife became pregnant roughly three months after our marriage. We still felt like strangers to each other being we had gotten married after only knowing each other for three months and now, three months later we had begun the process of having our first child together. My wife did have two boys from her first marriage. They were 5 and 6 years old when we got married. We were living in my parent's house at the time. My parents had two extra bedrooms, we converted one bedroom for the boys and put a crib in our bedroom. Me and my wife asked God for twins. When we went to an ultrasound, we discovered that there were indeed twins in my wife but that one had not survived. They asked us if we wanted to know the sexes of our twins. We told them that we did not want to know what the one was that didn't survive but we did want to know what we were having. I told my wife it didn't matter what we were going to have, but secretively, I was hoping for a boy. I hadn't thought too much about what sex our child would be, I was just so excited that I was finally going to have a child of my own. I had dreamed of having children as early as the age of 17. I wanted to be a young parent, and now I was 35 years old, twice the age I wanted to be having my first child.

When they told us it was going to be a girl my heart sank a little. It was only moments prior that I started to deeply think about how nice it would be to have a boy. But I tried to hide my hurt the best I could and was still excited.

We named our girl Vaybreein. Once we had her, she won my heart and when my wife got pregnant again, I really wanted another girl because of her. But God often does things the opposite of what I hope for or think he should. God does what is best for us. We had saved all of Vaybreein's clothes in case we had another girl, it would be very convenient to pass hers' down to our new child, but, we were now told we were having a boy. We named the boy Thayvin, and he has won my heart as well. The Bible is correct when it says that children are a blessing from the Lord. The Bible is also correct when it says, he that finds a wife, finds a good thing. Our biggest problem at the time was that we were now outgrowing my parents' house. We moved the boys down into the basement and made their room the younger children's room.

The boys seemed to like moving further away from us, but my wife did not like that they were now sleeping two stories away. We tried to find a place to rent or a bank to give us a loan to buy a house but struck out everywhere we went. My wife had bad credit, and I had no credit. Neither of us had any renter's history, and I had three felonies. As God is faithful though, we heard of a place called Habitat for Humanity. We moved into my wife's parents' house where we had more room for our expanding family. Thayvin was born while we lived there. We went from my parents' house in the city to my wife's parents' house which was in the country.

Chapter 65
"Habitat for Humanity"

We signed up to get a house through Habitat and were told that it would be a yearlong process. It ended up taking us three years to get into a house instead of only one year. This was because Habitat took on a big project right in the heart of my hometown. Habitat was planning on building ten houses in a small community area. These houses were going to have the best of the newest technology. The entire house would be run off of electricity and have 24 solar panels on the roof. Keeping the utility bills low would make it much more practical for families that were near the poverty level to afford these houses.

Overall, Habitat for Humanity is a great non-profit organization. It works off the belief that God wants us to help our neighbors in need. Habitat has a saying that they, "Offer a hand up, not a hand out". You are required to put in nearly 300 hours of labor each before moving into your new house. You still get a mortgage, but it is interest-free. That is the best benefit you get from habitat. Interest on a house mortgage is usually very costly. With this new solar panel technology, the cost for electrical and heating is supposed to be nothing. We were very confused when we got a utility bill for $150 our second month living in our new house. Come to find out, $60 a month goes to pay for our water and sewer. Overall, the solar panels are a blessing. They certainly keep the price of our utilities down. I did the math and discovered that we basically pay $30 a month for electricity after averaging it out for a year. In the winter we may pay $130 in a month but in the summer, get a credit for over $70.

We almost did not get our house. My wife had quit her job so that she could raise our four children, and I had gotten an incredible raise at my work. We had the same amount of income as we did before, but I was starting to take extra days off of work to help Habitat make certain deadlines they had to meet with their building project. My wife and I had already fulfilled our required number of hours needed to get our house, but I felt I would keep helping out anyways. This almost came back to bite me in the butt.

One week before we were supposed to sign the paperwork/mortgage for our new house, Habitat called us into their office and told us that we no longer qualified for the house we helped build. I did the math repeatedly and discovered that at the most, we were $50 short a month from qualifying. I was so angry that they were doing this to us. $50 was nothing. I made more than that in tips each month, and that was not even 3 hours of work at my job. I had taken up to 30 hours off of work in the last month in order to help Habitat. I felt like they were going to punish us for helping them. One time I helped them was when I called an old friend up who came over and finished our house's rough framing of our roof. Regular volunteers were not allowed to work on the roof. A person had to have their own contractor's license and insurance in order to work on the roofs of these new two-story houses. I could help my friend from down below by cutting the boards and handing them up to him, but I myself could not go up on the roof.

I contacted the head of our Habitat for Humanity's board and explained that I was making enough money, that the only reason I did not for that one month was because I took off an extra 30 hours to help them. He said we could find a solution. My wife suggested that we come up with a down payment on the house. He told me that if we could come up with $15,000 cash in a week, we could still get into our house. How is a family in poverty supposed to come up with $15,000 in a week? God is good though and we had 3 people who were even more mad at Habitat than us who were willing to give us money. We accepted my mother-in-law's help and she paid the $15,000 for us. We paid her back $5,000 a few months later when we got tax return money, but she told us we didn't have to pay back the other $10,000. It was just so frustrating to have been in the Habitat program for over 3 years to be told just a week before moving in that we no longer qualified.

Long story short, we moved into our new house on Thanksgiving Day. What a thing to be thankful for. I was now thirty-nine years old and finally moving out on my own with a wife and four children. I can't speak highly enough of Habitat, I am just not very pleased with some of the red tape and things they have done to us at the administration level. The true backbone and best part of Habitat, are the people who actually build the houses.

Habitat also disappointed me by the countless things they promised us only to have them not follow through with them. They started an association for our community and told us that the $25 association fee we each pay every month would cover a community trash can, lawn care, snow removal, etc. We have now paid our association fees for three years, and the only thing we have seen come from it is that our underground sprinkler water bill is paid for. These sprinklers come on way too often in the summer, and it looks like they have caused some sort of fungus to grow in our lawns that has killed most of the grass.

We never got a community trash can, never got lawn care, never got snow removal and now they raised the amount to almost double. We now pay $45 a month, $540 a year, and all we get is our grass watered for 4 months. The silly thing is, it only costs me $5 a month to water my small yard by hand. Like I said, I can't speak highly enough of Habitat itself, just some of the things they do frustrate you. Making promises and then not fulfilling them gets old after a while. There were countless of other promises they made that they also never went through with. But it sure is a blessing to have a forty-year loan and not have to pay interest on it. Our house payments are less expensive than our taxes and the insurance on our house. Part of that is because of how high taxes are in my city.

One last thing about our house that is a mixed blessing, is its location. We are right downtown and can walk to the beaches, stores, parks, library, river, etc. It is also only three blocks away from the house I lived in from the ages of 5 to 15.

The downfall is that we live just yards away from two bars and the loud noise from the bars are often a nuisance. It is mostly the people leaving the one bar at 2 am screaming, fighting, revving their engines, honking their horns, etc. Our neighbors, on the other hand, are some of the best people I have ever met. We are truly blessed to know each one of them on a close personal basis.

Chapter 66
"Still Pursuing Justice"

I do not feel like I have closure to the injustice I have suffered by going to prison for over 12 years for a crime I did not commit. I have recently sent the prosecutor a letter asking him to exonerate me and to compensate me. I enclosed with the letter the news article about how the FBI used bogus hair evidence for over two decades to falsely convict people as well as an article that states Michigan has made a law to compensate people who falsely get sent to prison $50,000 for each year they were unjustly locked up. I hand delivered a copy of what I sent the prosecutor to our local sheriff as well as to the FBI.

A month later I sent another letter to the prosecutor, sheriff, and FBI again asking to be exonerated and compensated. I also included copies of Priest's written statement stating that he heard Demon confess to the crime, as well as medical reports that shows Demon sustained injuries during the crash that prove he was indeed the driver. Thus far, I have not heard back from the prosecutor.

Apparently, he does not want to admit they threw me in prison for a crime I did not commit. I only asked him for $50,000 for each year I was locked up unjustly, the amount the law says they owe me. I have recently read a news article where a guy who was falsely sent to prison for a crime he did not commit based on bogus hair evidence, is suing the prosecutor and the town he is from for 4 million dollars for each year he was unjustly locked up. That is 80 times more than what I asked the prosecutor for. I am now presently looking for legal counsel but have not been very successful.

The prosecutor is running a campaign in hopes of becoming a judge in my town. Ironically, he is trying to win the very seat on the bench that my judge once held. He has not as much lifted a little finger to correct the injustice done to me. He has not been a good prosecutor and should not be a judge. I think he should step down from being a prosecutor, or at least do something to fix the injustice done to me.

Chapter 67
"Venting, Reward and Plea"

Since being released from prison, I have encountered a handful of people who also say they heard Demon confess to being the driver. Apparently, Priest is not the only one Demon confided in. Most of the guys are too scared to come forth because they are afraid of our police and judicial system. It isn't right when our government has us afraid to tell the truth or to come forward with evidence that proves an innocent man went to prison for over 12 years. One women told me that Demon's mom confided in her mom that she knows her son was driving.

I have also come across articles in the press that reveal that hair evidence has been used to falsely convict other people, that it is not a reliable evidence. I have also discovered that my state, The State of Michigan, has decided to compensate people $50,000 per year who have been wrongly imprisoned. Thus far, my state has not even given me as much as an apology for what they did to me. It seems according to their own law, the least amount that they owe me is $600,000 since I did over 12 years unjustly. (12 years x $50,000 = $600,000). I will give a **handsome reward** to someone if they come forth and testify against Demon. If their testimony results in me getting $600,000, I would have no problem giving them a **handsome reward**. I think it would be best for Demon to come forth himself and get it off his chest once and for all. He still has an opportunity to right a wrong here. The way I figure it, he (you) owe me this. Talk about a guilty conscience! Can you imagine what it must feel like for Demon knowing he sent an innocent man to prison for something he did? Put yourself in his shoes for a moment. I for one, would certainly come clean and fess up to what I did. But some people in this world don't have much of a conscience, I suppose, and are so selfish they only ever think of themselves.

Another way the truth could get out, and The State of Michigan could reward me the hundreds of thousands of dollars is if the DA would simply charge Demon and overturn my case. I am certain judges have the power to overturn my case, and I know that the DA has a large amount of power as well. After all, there are physical evidences that prove Demon was the driver of the car. The type of hair evidence that the FBI and Justice Department admits is bogus, was used in my case.

The DA has plenty of grounds to do what is right and just even without someone else coming forth to testify against Demon. I'm not sure how a DA can even live with a bad conscience of charging a 17-year-old with a crime he did not commit and then sending him away for 12 years at age 21. Maybe if any of you reading this book were to write the DA and tell him that he should clear my record and compensate me, the DA would do something. Sort of a power of the people type of thing.

If you feel like writing the DA, here is his address: (Update: Bob is now a judge)

Bob Cooney

324 Court Street

Traverse City, MI. 49684

I included an article at the end of this book by the Washington Post that talks about how the FBI and Department of Justice admit that the type of hair evidence they used in my case is a lie, that it misleads jurists, and that they have used it to convict people falsely. I am one of the people who was falsely convicted by bogus hair evidence, but no one has reviewed my case. In my case, the hair evidence was certainly used to trick the jury into believing I was the driver of the car when I was not. My trial judge even leaned on the bogus hair evidence when he ruled on my appeal based on newly discovered evidence; Demon's confession to Priest. He stated that it didn't matter that Demon confessed to Priest because there was hair evidence that proved I was guilty. It is obvious that the unreliable hair evidence not only convinced/deceived a jury to convict me of a crime I am innocent of, but it also fooled my trial judge as well.

One way they determine if a person should be exonerated of a crime is they analyze the case to determine if in a new trial the person would still possibly be found guilty. In my situation, there is no way I would be found guilty. There is legitimate physical evidence that proves Demon was the driver, the hair evidence has been declared inadmissible in court because of how faulty and misleading it is, and oh yeah, Demon has admitted that he was the driver.

Chapter 68
CIU (Conviction Integrity Unit)

In April of 2019, only a few months into her first term as The Attorney General of the State of Michigan, Dana Nessel, started a Conviction Integrity Unit (CIU). Shortly after hearing about this awesome new unit, I filled out an application to get my situation before them. As stated online; The CIU's, 'mission is to determine whether new evidence shows that an innocent person has been convicted of a crime, and to recommend steps to rectify such situations.'

As I stated earlier in this book, there are individuals who say they have heard Demon confess to the crime. One of them has since passed away, two others, are too scared of our government to come forward, especially after they saw what happened to me, but I have heard of others besides these three. I have made them aware of this, but thus far, over 5 years later, they have not done anything.

Another piece of evidence, never presented in court, is in regard to the bogus hair evidence used against me. This evidence, now considered unreliable and misleading, is no longer used in criminal cases. In my application to the Conviction Integrity Unit (CIU), I explained that the only evidence used to convict me was the testimony of two lying witnesses and this unreliable hair evidence. I also presented four pieces of physical evidence that prove Demon was the driver, and I explained how Demon confessed to the crime. This should be a straightforward case, easily resolved. Most people that I talk to or have read my book, are outraged by what happened and want to see me exonerated and compensated. If I were in a position of power, I would want to make things right. However, I worry that those in positions of power don't share the same sense of fairness and compassion that most of us ordinary people do.

My case was sent to the Thomas Cooley Law School's Innocent Research Project. This is the third time I've been involved with this project at the same school. Right away, they started giving me the same old runaround, focusing only on DNA evidence. I tried to explain that my case was about more than just DNA, and how disappointed I was with their approach. They always say they don't see any evidence, even though I've explained my case to kids as young as seven, and even they understand that I was clearly treated unfairly.

It seems like some institutions and people in power have gotten good at spinning things. They make excuses, change the subject, or make promises they never keep. It's like they're trying to avoid taking any real action. I recently heard back from The Innocent Project, and as expected, they said the same thing. There is no DNA evidence.

There never was. What there is though, is physical evidence that proves Demon was the driver, a confession made by him, and proof that bogus misleading evidence was used to falsely convict me.

I learned that a group of Michigan's political leaders were coming to my town, Traverse City, on August 23rd, 2019, to discuss our judicial system. They were specifically focusing on pretrial incarceration, and they were allowing people from the public to speak.

Since I spent almost four years on bond for a crime I didn't commit, I felt I had something important to say. When someone is first charged with a crime, authorities decide if they should be released on bond until their trial and there are a set of rules they need to adhere to. The problem is, they often have too much power. How can you punish someone like they did me when they're supposed to be considered innocent until proven guilty?

My bond was full of rules and restrictions. It's amazing I managed to follow them as well as I did. They controlled every minute of my life. I had to do whatever they said. I had to take breathalyzers at the police station every morning (365 days a year), attend college or work full-time, go to AA meetings, and take drug tests in the evening. I couldn't drive, not even a moped, and had an early curfew. I basically had to hitchhike 15 miles in and out of town up to four times a day just to comply with everything they demanded. I stood before these state leaders, including the Attorney General, the Lieutenant Governor, the Chief Justice of our state's supreme court, and several others. I didn't really know who they were at the time. I was hoping to speak directly to the Attorney General, but she had someone representing her.

I gave each of them a copy of this book you're reading now and explained how I had been wronged. I told them that even while I was on bond, having my name dragged through the mud by society, God was writing my name in the sky out of clouds. I explained more about my situation, how it's almost unheard of for someone to spend nearly four years on bond before going to trial. I enjoyed sharing my story with those in power.

I later found out they were going to be in a bigger city about two hours away from mine. I went there to speak to them again, hoping to address the Attorney General directly. But once again, she had someone else there in her place. However, I was surprised when the guy representing her secretly met with me in the hallway and told me she was aware of my case and that I should be patient.

That was over five years ago. I don't have much patience left. Enough is enough. This injustice has continued for over 30 years. The man who killed three teenagers has never spent a single day in jail for it. Instead, he was given almost fifty thousand dollars. Talk about injustice! And I'm still suffering from all of this. I can't seem to get a decent job. I still struggle with post-traumatic stress and depression from everything I went through. I try to focus on the positive things in my life, but it's hard to ignore the fact that they know I am innocent and yet refuse to do anything about it. They have the power to fix this, but until now they have not done anything. Any decent human being would have already done so.

I know ultimately God will give me justice and compensate me, but that doesn't excuse those who are refusing to do what they can to make things right.

If you've read this far, you're likely a decent person. Even if you don't think you're significant or a great communicator, I need your help. I'm calling for action! I'm asking for reader participation!

Chapter 69
A Call to Action/Reader Participation

The very least you can do is pray for me. Another thing you can do is write a letter to the authorities expressing your thoughts on how my case should be handled. Even a short note would make a difference.

Do you think I should be given $50,000 for each year I was unjustly behind bars? Or should I get millions for them taking away my 16 most prime years (17-33 years old)? That includes the four years I spent under their thumb while on bond having to do everything they said! Often those 4 years were worse than the time I spent in prison. What about all the years I have had to spend after prison with felony convictions on my record that should not have been there? I have been out of prison now for over 15 years but still suffer because I am labeled a felon. They made it very difficult to get my driver's license back. And I pretty much only get the bottom of the barrel jobs that no one else really wants.

Put yourself in my shoes and express yourself to these people in power and tell them you feel that they should exonerate and compensate me. Should they clear my record and give me a million dollars? Should they give me 10 million dollars for basically controlling and destroying my life for over 30 years? Or should they give me 100 million dollars? What would you want if they did all of this to you? I have recently asked them for 22 million dollars. 1 million for each year they punished me unjustly, and 2 million for the last 6 years I spent behind bars even after the confession came out.

You can email your letter to the Attorney General, to the local prosecutor in my town, to the Michigan State Police, The FBI or even the president of the United States, or to each and every one of them. Their email addresses are as follows:

- Attorney General's Assistant, Lori Montgomery: MontgomeryL4@michigan.gov
- Michigan Attorney General, Danna Nessel: miag@michigan.gov
- Grand Traverse Prosecutor, Noelle Moeggenburg: nmoeggen@gtcontymi.gov
- President Trump: Just google "Contact President Trump." He has his own website.
- Michigan State Police: They also have their own email and website.

Maybe you can think of someone else to write or contact that can help make this wrong done to me right.

There is something seriously wrong when the judicial system can get away with something like this.

The man who killed three teenagers was allowed to lie on the stand and blame me. He'd already changed his story to the police four times, that alone showed suspicion that he was the guilty one. There's clear physical evidence he was the driver, including matching injuries and car damage. He even confessed to being the driver! He was granted nearly $50,000, money meant for the victims' families. He killed three children and then stole from their parents. He crashed my car, almost killed me, and sent me to prison for it.

The judicial system has never even made him spend a single day in jail for any of this. While the deaths were accidental, his actions after the crash were not. It is easier to forgive or justify things people do on accident, but when they purposely and beforehand plan them out, that is a different story and is a more serious crime. He lied about injuries, stole money, and framed me, all those acts were deliberate and malicious.

The injustice continues. The families deserve closure, and I deserve relief. Demon should face consequences for his actions. If Demon had admitted his guilt from the start, he could have taken a plea deal and served a few months in jail. He wasn't drunk driving, so he wouldn't have faced the same charges as me. He could have simply expressed remorse and accepted responsibility. Instead, I spent four years on bond, twelve years in prison, and I'm still suffering.

Even now, they could charge Demon, offer him a plea bargain, and resolve this quickly. I'm writing to the local authorities, including the new Sheriff, prosecuting attorney, President Trump, and I'll contact the Attorney General again.

Please join me in writing to them as well. It's a small request, but it could make a big difference.

If you can't write a quick email to help me, please spread the word about my story. Tell people about the injustice I've faced. I'm using book sales to start "Club JESUS" and hope to make a movie about my experience to further expose the corruption in our judicial system while spreading the gospel of Jesus Christ!

Wouldn't you feel good knowing you helped get me justice? It's a small act of kindness that can make a big difference. It only takes a few minutes to write an email to our government officials demanding they make things right. We need to hold them accountable. Share my story with your local media or on social media – even if you only have a few followers.

The media betrayed me. They declared me guilty before my trial, influencing potential jurors. I'm grateful for social media, which can't be controlled like mainstream media. They've been spreading fake news long before President Trump called it that. I saw it firsthand in 1993 when they started falsely accusing me.

I cannot say this enough, ENOUGH IS ENOUGH, and I need your help! Let's clean up our corrupt judicial system! We the people want a fair and just system. These people in power work for us. They are of the people, by the people and for the people. Let's tell them to do what is in our best interest or else resign. We the people need to rise up together. I cannot do this on my own.

God Bless You!

And God Bless America!!!

Jash Eli Lardie.

Chapter 70
"Conclusion"

This pretty much sums up my life's story. I did leave a lot of stuff out only because I feel like this book would be twice the size it is if I had not, and besides, it leaves room for a sequel.

The main thing I have learned is that God is only a prayer away from us. I encourage everyone to call on the name of Jesus and see just how near he is. Call from a pure heart though, those who call on him as an arrogant and proud enemy of his won't experience him in the same loving way that those who approach him in humbleness do. The best thing you can do is turn from your sins by asking him to forgive you and be your Lord and Savior, then you will see that God is the most loving of fathers. He is our Father, who art in heaven, once we become born again as his children.

My hope and prayer is that God plants a seed of faith and hope in your heart from reading my testimony. Countless of times I have told people the stories about how I got saved in an all-black church down south, and about how God wrote my name in the sky out of clouds, only to watch those people call out to God themselves and then come back to me to tell me how God showed up in their lives as well. I hope you become one of those people also. Going to prison for 12 years was not all fun and games, but I am certain that it is far better than going to hell for all of eternity. I can't stress enough that both God and I want you to go to heaven and that you should make sure you are going there when you die as soon as possible because you do not know the day or hour that you will die, or when Christ may return.

Believe it or not, there are days when I miss prison. Prison was a taste of hell many of the days I was there, but I often found myself pressing deeper into the love of God and discovered that even during the worst of days (our darkest hours), He gives you a peace that passes understanding and a joy that is indescribable and full of glory.

I included a prayer of salvation that anyone who wants to experience the true goodness of God can pray. The exact words you pray are not what is most important. What is important, is that you let him come into your heart as Lord, Savior, Father, and friend!

God Bless You!

Jash E. Lardie.

Prayer of Salvation

Dear Lord Jesus, I (say your name) believe you died for me. Forgive me my sins. Come into my heart, into my life, and fill me with your spirit. I accept you, Jesus Christ as my personal Lord and Savior!

Amen!

The following is a copy of the Washington Post's article about how hair evidence is bogus and has been used to falsely convict many people.

FBI admits flaws in hair analysis over decades

The Washington Post

By Spencer S. Hsu By Spencer S. Hsu

Local

April 18, 2015

The Justice Department and FBI have formally acknowledged that nearly every examiner in an elite FBI forensic unit gave flawed testimony in almost all trials in which they offered evidence against criminal defendants over more than a two-decade period before 2000.

Of 28 examiners with the FBI Laboratory's microscopic hair comparison unit, 26 overstated forensic matches in ways that favored prosecutors in more than 95 percent of the 268 trials reviewed so far, according to the National Association of Criminal Defense Lawyers (NACDL) and the Innocence Project, which are assisting the government with the country's largest post-conviction review of questioned forensic evidence.

The cases include those of 32 defendants sentenced to death. Of those, 14 have been executed or died in prison, the groups said under an agreement with the government to release results after the review of the first 200 convictions.

The FBI errors alone do not mean there was not other evidence of a convict's guilt. Defendants and federal and state prosecutors in 46 states and the District are being notified to determine whether there are grounds for appeals. Four defendants were previously exonerated.

The admissions mark a watershed in one of the country's largest forensic scandals, highlighting the failure of the nation's courts for decades to keep bogus scientific information from juries, legal analysts said. The question now, they said, is how state authorities and the courts will respond to findings that confirm long-suspected problems with subjective, pattern-based forensic techniques — like hair and bite-mark comparisons — that have contributed to wrongful convictions in more than one-quarter of 329 DNA-exoneration cases since 1989.

In a statement, the FBI and Justice Department vowed to continue to devote resources to address all cases and said they "are committed to ensuring that affected defendants are notified of past errors and that justice is done in every instance. The Department and the FBI are also committed to ensuring the accuracy of future hair analysis testimony, as well as the application of all disciplines of forensic science."

Peter Neufeld, co-founder of the Innocence Project, commended the FBI and department for the collaboration but said, "The FBI's three-decade use of microscopic hair analysis to incriminate defendants was a complete disaster."

"We need an exhaustive investigation that looks at how the FBI, state governments that relied on examiners trained by the FBI and the courts allowed this to happen and why it wasn't stopped much sooner," Neufeld said.

Norman L. Reimer, the NACDL's executive director, said, "Hopefully, this project establishes a precedent so that in future situations it will not take years to remediate the injustice."

While unnamed federal officials previously acknowledged widespread problems, the FBI until now has withheld comment because findings might not be representative.

Sen. Richard Blumenthal (D-Conn.), a former prosecutor, called on the FBI and Justice Department to notify defendants in all 2,500 targeted cases involving an FBI hair match about the problem even if their case has not been completed, and to redouble efforts in the three-year-old review to retrieve information on each case.

"These findings are appalling and chilling in their indictment of our criminal justice system, not only for potentially innocent defendants who have been wrongly imprisoned and even executed, but for prosecutors who have relied on fabricated and false evidence despite their intentions to faithfully enforce the law," Blumenthal said.

Senate Judiciary Committee Chairman Charles E. Grassley (R-Iowa) and the panel's ranking Democrat, Patrick J. Leahy (Vt.), urged the bureau to conduct "a root-cause analysis" to prevent future breakdowns.

"It is critical that the Bureau identify and address the systemic factors that allowed this far-reaching problem to occur and continue for more than a decade," the lawmakers wrote FBI Director James B. Comey on March 27, as findings were being finalized.

The FBI is waiting to complete all reviews to assess causes but has acknowledged that hair examiners until 2012 lacked written standards defining scientifically appropriate and erroneous ways to explain results in court. The bureau expects this year to complete similar standards for testimony and lab reports for 19 forensic disciplines.

Federal authorities launched the investigation in 2012 after The Washington Post reported that flawed forensic hair matches might have led to the convictions of hundreds of potentially innocent people since at least the 1970s, typically for murder, rape and other violent crimes nationwide.

The review confirmed that FBI experts systematically testified to the near-certainty of "matches" of crime-scene hairs to defendants, backing their claims by citing incomplete or misleading statistics drawn from their case work.

In reality, there is no accepted research on how often hair from different people may appear the same. Since 2000, the lab has used visual hair comparison to rule out someone as a possible source of hair or in combination with more accurate DNA testing.

Warnings about the problem have been mounting. In 2002, the FBI reported that its own DNA testing found that examiners reported false hair matches more than 11 percent of the time. In the District, the only jurisdiction where defenders and prosecutors have re-investigated all FBI hair convictions, three of seven defendants whose trials included flawed FBI testimony have been exonerated through DNA testing since 2009, and courts have exonerated two more men. All five served 20 to 30 years in prison for rape or murder.

University of Virginia law professor Brandon L. Garrett said the results reveal a "mass disaster" inside the criminal justice system, one that it has been unable to self-correct because courts rely on outdated precedents admitting scientifically invalid testimony at trial and, under the legal doctrine of finality, make it difficult for convicts to challenge old evidence.

"The tools don't exist to handle systematic errors in our criminal justice system," Garrett said. "The FBI deserves every recognition for doing something really remarkable here. The problem is there may be few judges, prosecutors or defense lawyers who are able or willing to do anything about it."

Federal authorities are offering new DNA testing in cases with errors, if sought by a judge or prosecutor, and agreeing to drop procedural objections to appeals in federal cases.

However, biological evidence in the cases often is lost or unavailable. Among states, only California and Texas specifically allow appeals when experts recant or scientific advances undermine forensic evidence at trial.

Defense attorneys say scientifically invalid forensic testimony should be considered as violations of due process, as courts have held with false or misleading testimony.

The FBI searched more than 21,000 federal and state requests to its hair comparison unit from 1972 through 1999, identifying for review roughly 2,500 cases where examiners declared hair matches.

Reviews of 342 defendants' convictions were completed as of early March, the NACDL and Innocence Project reported. In addition to the 268 trials in which FBI hair evidence was used against defendants, the review found cases in which defendants pleaded guilty, FBI examiners did not testify, did not assert a match or gave exculpatory testimony.

When such cases are included, by the FBI's count examiners made statements exceeding the limits of science in about 90 percent of testimonies, including 34 death-penalty cases.

The findings likely scratch the surface. The FBI said as of mid-April that reviews of about 350 trial testimonies and 900 lab reports are nearly complete, with about 1,200 cases remaining.

The bureau said it is difficult to check cases before 1985, when files were computerized. It has been unable to review 700 cases because police or prosecutors did not respond to requests for information.

Also, the same FBI examiners whose work is under review taught 500 to 1,000 state and local crime lab analysts to testify in the same ways.

Texas, New York and North Carolina authorities are reviewing their hair examiner cases, with ad hoc efforts underway in about 15 other states.

This was the prison I was at. Five stories of human sized bird cages.
Bogus hair evidence!!!

Wednesday
December 11, 1996

Scientist supports claims Lardie was driver

■ She testifies about hair fragments found on the car's windshield

By WILL SCOTT
Record-Eagle staff writer

TRAVERSE CITY — A forensic scientist's testimony Tuesday about hairs found in the windshield of Josh Lardie's car supported prosecutors' claims that Lardie was driving when the car crashed in May 1993.

Connie Swander, a scientist with the state police crime laboratory in Grayling, testified that hair fragments found on the passenger side of the windshield were similar to hair samples from [illegible] Timm.

Swander testified that other hair fragments, found left of the windshield's center, were similar to hair samples from Lardie.

The fragments that resembled Lardie's hair didn't resemble Timm's, and vice-versa, Swander said.

Lardie, 21, is accused of being the driver and being drunk when his 1987 Nissan Sentra crashed into a tree on Peninsula Drive May 23, 1993. The crash killed Jason Stutesman, Keadra Tiernan and Erinn Tompkins.

Lardie is charged with three counts of causing a death while driving drunk. If convicted, he could face up to 15 years in prison.

Grand Traverse County Assistant Prosecutor Robert Cooney all but wrapped up his case Tuesday, the trial's fifth day.

Because of scheduling conflicts, the trial won't resume until next Tuesday. Defense attorney Paul Scholtz will then present his opening witness and is expected to eventually call Lardie to the stand.

On Tuesday, Swander testified that she and county sheriff's detective Sgt. Mike Imhoff removed the hair fragments, all between one-quarter and three-eighths of an inch long, from the car's windshield. She said some of [illegible] fragments were embedded in the windshield, which had shattered but remained more or less in its original shape.

Detectives discovered the hair fragments in the windshield this fall, after prosecutors began focusing on the issue of whether Lardie had indeed been the driver.

Swander said she compared the hair fragments with roughly 100 hair samples each from Lardie and Timm.

Swander testified that she could not match a given hair to a single person, but she could eliminate people based on the characteristics of their hair.

Timm testified earlier that he has regularly bleached his hair for the past few years, but couldn't remember if his hair was bleached at the time of the crash. Swander testified Tuesday that even without considering color or chemical treatment, the hair fragments on the right side of the windshield were still similar to Timm's.

The case has been delayed about three years by challenges of the law under which Lardie was charged. The case was set for trial after the state Supreme Court ruled earlier this year that the law was constitutional.

The Driver's seat was bent around 18 inches in the right shoulder area.

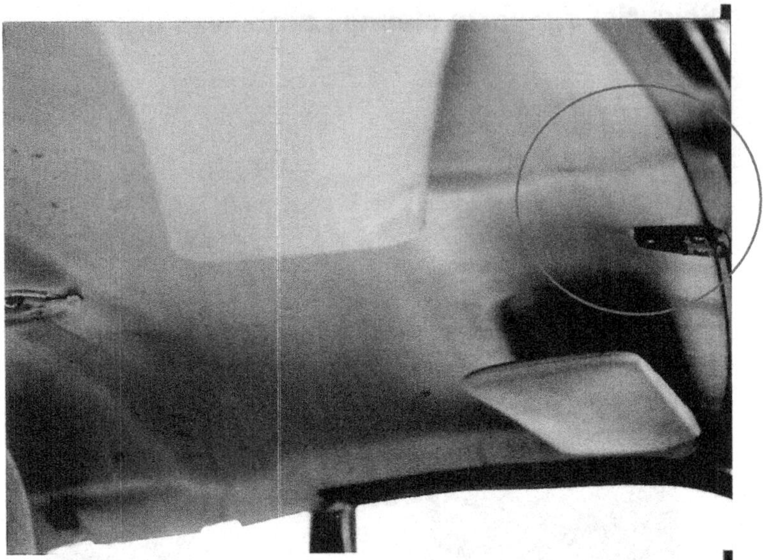

CFA 880

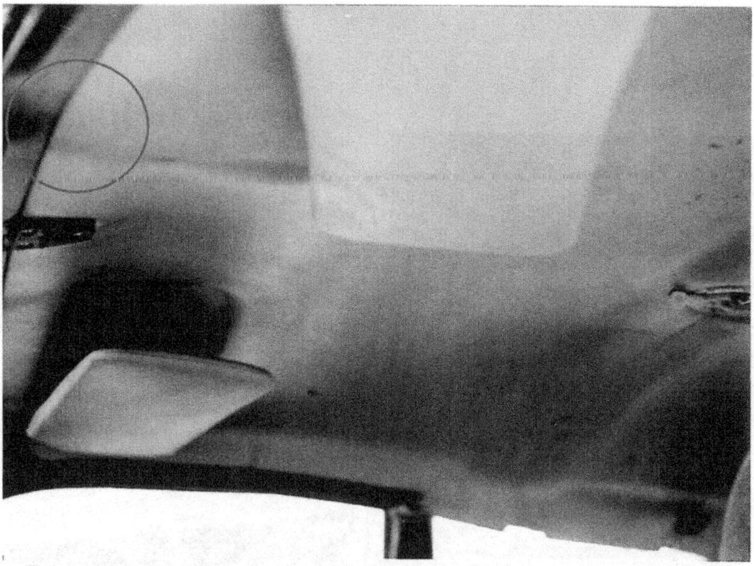

Dent in trim that expert witness testified was caused by the driver hitting their head.

Reverse image blown up. Actual dent is on the driver's side of the car, as shown in the image above.

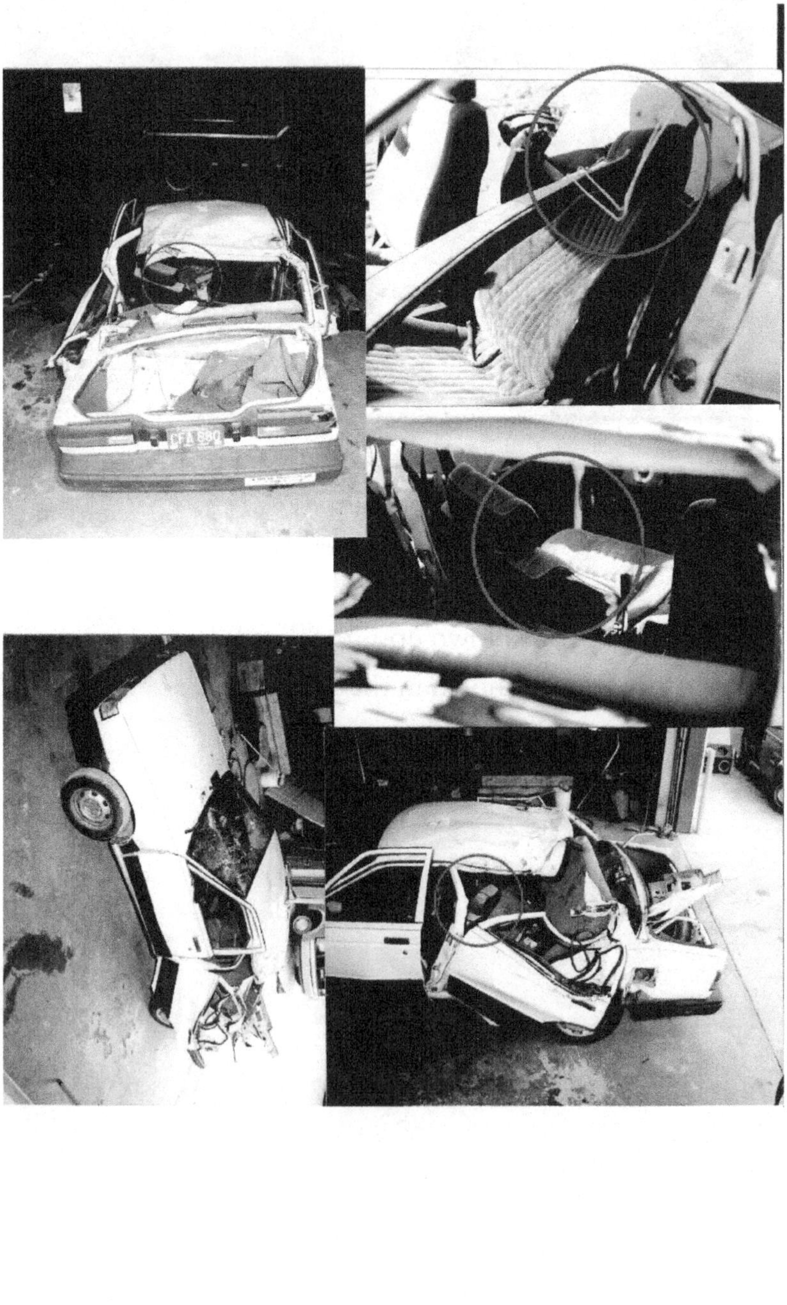

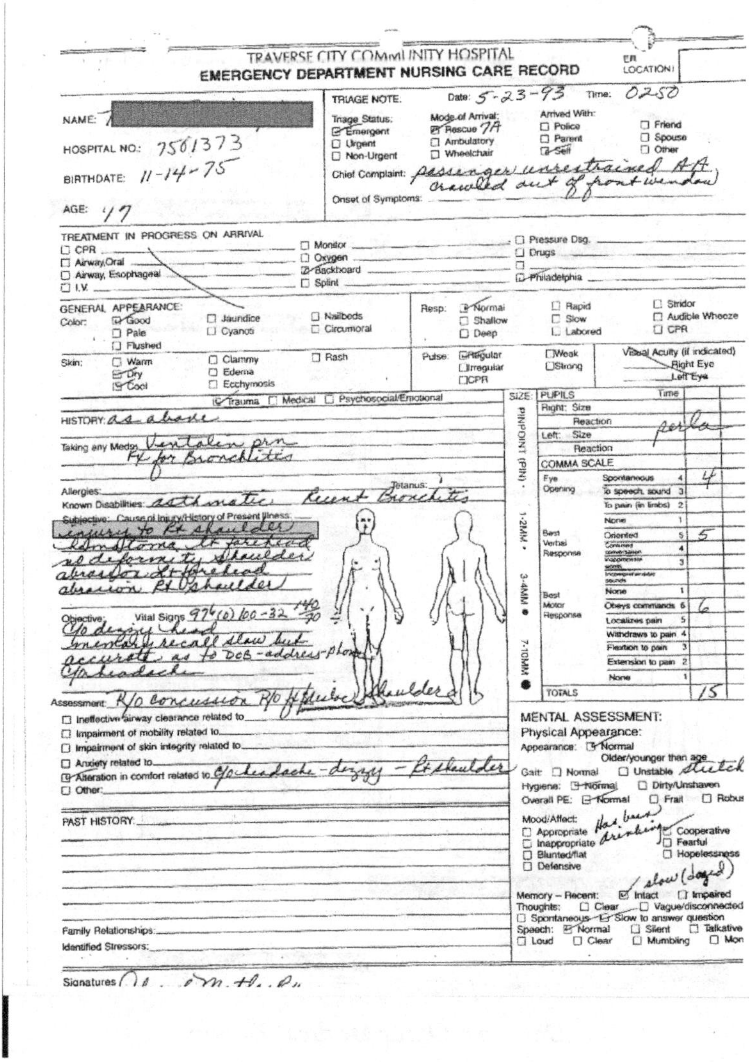

TRAVERSE CITY COMMUNITY HOSPITAL
EMERGENCY DEPARTMENT NURSING CARE RECORD

ER LOCATION:

NAME: [redacted]

HOSPITAL NO.: 7561373

BIRTHDATE: 11-14-75

AGE: 17

TRIAGE NOTE. Date: 5-23-93 Time: 0250

Triage Status: ☑ Emergent ☐ Urgent ☐ Non-Urgent

Mode of Arrival: ☑ Rescue 7A ☐ Ambulatory ☐ Wheelchair

Arrived With: ☐ Police ☐ Parent ☑ Self ☐ Friend ☐ Spouse ☐ Other

Chief Complaint: passenger unrestrained AA crawled out of front window

Onset of Symptoms:

TREATMENT IN PROGRESS ON ARRIVAL
☐ CPR ☐ Airway, Oral ☐ Airway, Esophageal ☐ I.V.
☐ Monitor ☐ Oxygen ☑ Backboard ☐ Splint
☐ Pressure Dsg. ☐ Drugs ☐ ☑ Philadelphia

GENERAL APPEARANCE:
Color: ☑ Good ☐ Pale ☐ Flushed ☐ Jaundice ☐ Cyanotic ☐ Nailbeds ☐ Circumoral
Skin: ☐ Warm ☑ Dry ☑ Cool ☐ Clammy ☐ Edema ☐ Ecchymosis ☐ Rash
Resp: ☑ Normal ☐ Shallow ☐ Deep ☐ Rapid ☐ Slow ☐ Labored ☐ Stridor ☐ Audible Wheeze ☐ CPR
Pulse: ☑ Regular ☐ Irregular ☐ CPR ☐ Weak ☐ Strong
Visual Acuity (if indicated) Right Eye Left Eye

☑ Trauma ☐ Medical ☐ Psychosocial/Emotional

HISTORY: as above

Taking any Meds: Ventolin prn Rx for Bronchitis

Allergies: Tetanus:

Known Disabilities: asthmatic Recent Bronchitis

Subjective: Cause of Injury/History of Present Illness: injury to Rt shoulder hematoma Lt forehead no deformity shoulder abrasion Lt forehead abrasion Rt shoulder

Objective: Vital Signs 97⁶(0) 100-32 140/90
C/o dizzy head
mentally recall slow but accurate as to DOB-address-phone
C/o headache

Assessment: R/O concussion R/O Rt Dislocated shoulder

☐ Ineffective airway clearance related to
☐ Impairment of mobility related to
☐ Impairment of skin integrity related to
☐ Anxiety related to
☑ Alteration in comfort related to C/o headache - dizzy - Rt shoulder
☐ Other:

PAST HISTORY:

Family Relationships:

Identified Stressors:

SIZE: PINPOINT (PIN) 1-2MM 3-4MM 7-10MM

PUPILS		Time
Right: Size		
Reaction		perla
Left: Size		
Reaction		

COMMA SCALE			
Eye Opening	Spontaneous	4	4
	To speech, sound	3	
	To pain (in limbs)	2	
	None	1	
Best Verbal Response	Oriented	5	5
	Confused conversation	4	
	Inappropriate words	3	
	Incomprehensible sounds	2	
	None	1	
Best Motor Response	Obeys commands	6	6
	Localizes pain	5	
	Withdraws to pain	4	
	Flexion to pain	3	
	Extension to pain	2	
	None	1	
TOTALS			15

MENTAL ASSESSMENT:
Physical Appearance:
Appearance: ☑ Normal Older/younger than age
Gait: ☐ Normal ☐ Unstable Stretch
Hygiene: ☑ Normal ☐ Dirty/Unshaven
Overall PE: ☑ Normal ☐ Frail ☐ Robust
Mood/Affect: Has been drinking
☐ Appropriate ☐ Inappropriate ☐ Blunted/flat ☐ Defensive ☑ Cooperative ☐ Fearful ☐ Hopelessness
slow (dazed)
Memory – Recent: ☑ Intact ☐ Impaired
Thoughts: ☐ Clear ☐ Vague/disconnected ☐ Spontaneous ☑ Slow to answer question
Speech: ☑ Normal ☐ Silent ☐ Talkative ☐ Loud ☐ Clear ☐ Mumbling ☐ Mon

Signatures

Demon's Medical Report

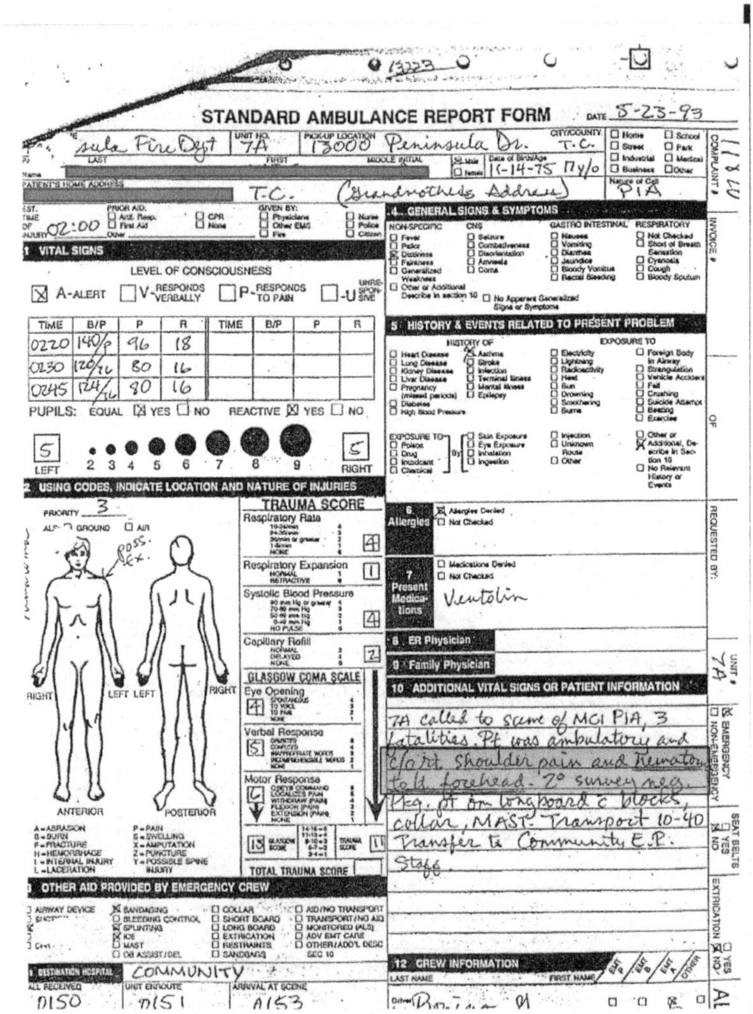

13223

STANDARD AMBULANCE REPORT FORM DATE 5-23-93

...sula Fire Dept | UNIT NO. 7A | PICK-UP LOCATION 13000 Peninsula Dr. | CITY/COUNTY T.C.

LAST | FIRST | MIDDLE INITIAL | ☒ Male ☐ Female | Date of Birth/Age 11-14-75 17 y/o

Name [redacted]

PATIENT'S HOME ADDRESS [redacted] T.C. (Grandmother's Address)

☐ Home ☐ School ☐ Street ☐ Park ☐ Industrial ☐ Medical ☐ Business ☐ Other

Nature of Call: PIA

EST. TIME OF INJURY 02:00

PRIOR AID: ☐ Artif. Resp. ☐ First Aid ☐ CPR ☐ None Other

GIVEN BY: ☐ Physicians ☐ Other EMS ☐ Fire ☐ Nurse ☐ Police ☐ Citizen

1 VITAL SIGNS

LEVEL OF CONSCIOUSNESS

☒ A-ALERT ☐ V-RESPONDS VERBALLY ☐ P-RESPONDS TO PAIN ☐ -U UNRESPONSIVE

TIME	B/P	P	R	TIME	B/P	P	R
0220	140/?	96	18				
0230	120/76	80	16				
0245	124/76	80	16				

PUPILS: EQUAL ☒ YES ☐ NO REACTIVE ☒ YES ☐ NO

LEFT 5 — 2 3 4 5 6 7 8 9 — RIGHT 5

2 USING CODES, INDICATE LOCATION AND NATURE OF INJURIES

PRIORITY 3

ALS ☐ GROUND ☐ AIR

poss. fx.

RIGHT LEFT LEFT RIGHT

ANTERIOR POSTERIOR

A = ABRASION, B = BURN, F = FRACTURE, H = HEMORRHAGE, I = INTERNAL INJURY, L = LACERATION, P = PAIN, S = SWELLING, X = AMPUTATION, Z = PUNCTURE, Y = POSSIBLE SPINE INJURY

TRAUMA SCORE

Respiratory Rate 4

Respiratory Expansion 1

Systolic Blood Pressure 4

Capillary Refill 2

GLASGOW COMA SCALE

Eye Opening 4

Verbal Response 5

Motor Response 6

GLASGOW SCORE 15 TRAUMA SCORE 11

TOTAL TRAUMA SCORE

3 OTHER AID PROVIDED BY EMERGENCY CREW

☐ AIRWAY DEVICE ☐ SUCTION ☒ BANDAGING ☐ BLEEDING CONTROL ☒ SPLINTING ☒ ICE ☐ MAST ☐ OB ASSIST/DEL ☐ COLLAR ☐ SHORT BOARD ☐ LONG BOARD ☐ EXTRICATION ☐ RESTRAINTS ☐ SANDBAGS ☐ AID/NO TRANSPORT ☐ TRANSPORT/NO AID ☐ MONITORED (ALS) ☐ ADV EMT CARE ☐ OTHER/ADD'L DESC SEC 10

DESTINATION HOSPITAL: COMMUNITY

CALL RECEIVED 0150 | UNIT ENROUTE 0151 | ARRIVAL AT SCENE 0153

4 GENERAL SIGNS & SYMPTOMS

NON-SPECIFIC: ☐ Fever ☐ Pallor ☒ Dizziness ☐ Faintness ☐ Generalized Weakness ☐ Other or Additional Describe in section 10

CNS: ☐ Seizure ☐ Combativeness ☐ Disorientation ☐ Amnesia ☐ Coma

☐ No Apparent Generalized Signs or Symptoms

GASTRO INTESTINAL: ☐ Nausea ☐ Vomiting ☐ Diarrhea ☐ Jaundice ☐ Bloody Vomitus ☐ Rectal Bleeding

RESPIRATORY: ☐ Not Checked ☐ Short of Breath Sensation ☐ Cyanosis ☐ Cough ☐ Bloody Sputum

5 HISTORY & EVENTS RELATED TO PRESENT PROBLEM

HISTORY OF: ☐ Heart Disease ☐ Lung Disease ☐ Kidney Disease ☐ Liver Disease ☐ Pregnancy (missed periods) ☐ Diabetes ☐ High Blood Pressure ☒ Asthma ☐ Stroke ☐ Infection ☐ Terminal Illness ☐ Mental Illness ☐ Epilepsy

EXPOSURE TO: ☐ Electricity ☐ Lightning ☐ Radioactivity ☐ Heat ☐ Sun ☐ Drowning ☐ Smothering ☐ Burns ☐ Foreign Body in Airway ☐ Strangulation ☐ Vehicle Accident ☐ Fall ☐ Crushing ☐ Suicide Attempt ☐ Beating ☐ Exercise

EXPOSURE TO: ☐ Poison ☐ Drug ☐ Intoxicant ☐ Chemical — By: ☐ Skin Exposure ☐ Eye Exposure ☐ Inhalation ☐ Ingestion ☐ Injection ☐ Unknown Route ☐ Other

☐ Other or ☒ Additional, Describe in Section 10 ☐ No Relevant History or Events

6 Allergies ☒ Allergies Denied ☐ Not Checked

7 Present Medications ☐ Medications Denied ☐ Not Checked — Ventolin

8 ER Physician

9 Family Physician

10 ADDITIONAL VITAL SIGNS OR PATIENT INFORMATION

7A called to scene of MCI PIA, 3 fatalities. Pt was ambulatory and c/o rt shoulder pain and hematoma to lt forehead. 2° survey neg. Neg. Pt on longboard c blocks, collar, MAST. Transport 10-40 Transfer to Community E.P. Staff.

12 CREW INFORMATION

LAST NAME | FIRST NAME | EMT P | EMT B | EMT A | OTHER

COMPLAINT # | INVOICE # | OF | REQUESTED BY: | UNIT # 7A | ☒ EMERGENCY ☐ NON-EMERGENCY | SEAT BELTS ☐ YES ☐ NO | EXTRICATION ☐ YES ☒ NO

Demon's Other Medical Report

"THE POWER RODGERS HAS"

"A."

MCL 770.1 New trial; reasons for granting.

Sec. 1. The judge of a court in which the trial of an offense is held may grant a new trial to the defendant, for any cause for which by law a new trial may be granted, or when it appears to the court that justice has not been done, and on terms or conditions as the court directs.

770.1 note 91. Sufficiency of evidence, causes or grounds for new trial.

Where trial judge, if he had tried case without jury, could not have concluded that defendants were guilty beyond a reasonable doubt, grant of a new trial following jury verdict of guilty was not improper, under statute authorizing the court to grant a new trial to defendant for any cause for which by law a new trial may be granted or when it shall appear to the court that justice has not been done. People -v- Johnson (1974) 218 N.W. 2d 378, 391 Mich. 834, appeal after remand 242 N.W. 2d 35, 68 Mich. App. 54

New trial may be granted if trial judge finds that guilty verdict was not in accordance with evidence produced and that injustice has been done. People -v- Hence (1981) 312 N.W. 2d 191, 110 Mich. App. 154.

"B"

Head note number 3 in People -v- Johnson 68 Mich App 54 (1976) says, "A Supreme Court decision upholding a trial judge's order granting a new trial did not take away from the trial judge the power to enter an order of dismissal for the defendants at the new trial, where the same judge presided over both the old and the new trial and had entered the order for the new trial, following a jury verdict of guilty at the first trial, because he felt that some of the testimony presented by the prosecution at the first trial was not worthy of belief and where the prosecution has conceded that no new evidence will be forthcoming at the new trial."

pg. 60 "In the present case, although there is "sufficient evidence" to support a conviction, the trial court has ruled that some of the testimony was not worthy of belief and is in that sense insufficient. The Supreme Court has affirmed the grant of a new trial on that basis."

The Power A Judge Has

MI2812800 GRAND TRAVERSE COUNTY SHERIFF'S OFFICE
FILE CLASS: 93001 128-11820-93
SUPPLEMENT #121 BY TROMBLEY ON 3/31/2003 PAGE 1

TYPE OF INCIDENT:	OUIL/PIA DEATH INVESTIGATION
SUSPECT:	JASH LARDIE
WITNESS:	SHAWN PRIEST

INFORMATION:

On 3/24/03 I received a letter from Captain WOOTERS that was address to the Sheriff's Department regarding JASH LARDIE. The letter was from BARB LARDIE, the mother of JASH LARDIE and relayed information that her son RAMUS had spoken to an individual by the name of SHAWN PRIEST. PRIEST stated that CHRISTOPHER TIMM admitted that he was the driver the night of the OUIL/PIA.

I was instructed to contact PRIEST, reinterview him and provide the information to the Prosecutor for their review.

INTERVIEW SHAWN PRIEST:

I met twice with SHAWN PRIEST who currently resides at 1709 Allen Road in Traverse City. PRIEST also is employed at Minerva's Restaurant as a cook in the kitchen.

When I first met with PRIEST he advised that he was at the party at the LARDIE house on the night of the accident involving the three deaths. He stated that he had been questioned by a detective after the accident, however does not remember the information that he provided. PRIEST stated that in the fall of the year he and CHRISTOPHER TIMM moved out to Salt Lake Tahoe in Nevada where they were roommates with three other males. They all worked at a ski resort and sometime during the fall of that year, he remembers TIMM telling him that he was the driver of the vehicle on the night in question.

Due to the fact that PRIEST was working, I did not take up any more of his time and requested him to respond to the Department on the following day where we could have an in-depth interview and he could write out a written statement. MR. PRIEST agreed and on 3/26/03 PRIEST responded to the Sheriff's Department and our interview continued.

PRIEST was escorted to the interview room in the Detective Bureau where we sat down and discussed the circumstances surrounding CHRISTOPHER TIMM'S confession to him.

MI2812800 GRAND TRAVERSE COUNTY SHERIFF'S OFFICE
FILE CLASS: 93001 128-11820-93
SUPPLEMENT #121 BY TROMBLEY ON 3/31/2003 PAGE 2

PRIEST stated that he and CHRISTOPHER TIMM moved to South Lake Tahoe, Nevada in October of 1993. PRIEST stated that he stayed there until approximately April of 1994 when he returned back to Traverse City. He stated that TIMM stayed there and then sometime after that moved out to Vermont to an unknown location. PRIEST went on to state that he and CHRIS, along with two other males a DARREN SMITH and BRIAN FRUSTY, all lived together and worked at the Heavenly Hills Ski Resort. PRIEST stated that sometime in October or November of 1993, PRIEST had a collapsed lung and was bedridden, unable to work. He stated that one particular evening CHRISTOPHER TIMM came back to the apartment and appeared to be somewhat intoxicated. He advised that TIMM came into the apartment and began speaking with PRIEST. PRIEST advised that CHRIS sat down and said something to the fact that "I need to get something off my chest". He then went on to say, "I believe I was driving on the night of the accident".

SHAWN advised that he had asked CHRIS why he did not come forward at the time and TIMM began explaining that he was afraid to come forward because JASON STUTSMAN was his cousin and did not wish to put his family or the other families through anymore embarrassment or hassle. Also TIMM received a pretty hefty cash settlement from the accident and just before finishing the conversation, TIMM advised PRIEST to "just keep this between us".

In questioning PRIEST further, it does not appear that PRIEST has any motivation to fabricate this story or to try to implicate CHRIS TIMM. PRIEST advised that he has not seen TIMM since approximately 1994, nor has he had any contact with JASH LARDIE or the LARDIE family. He advised that he only recently ran into RAMUS LARDIE and provided RAMUS LARDIE with the information that he had from the fall of 1993.

In questioning PRIEST more about the reason he did not come forth earlier, PRIEST advised that he was a main provider of the beer and alcohol from the main house down to the bonfire where the juveniles and minors were gathered. PRIEST advised that he feared that he could possibly be charged and/or connected to the deaths and the accident for his part in providing the alcohol from the house.

After our conversation, I requested PRIEST to write out a written statement, which he did and that statement will be attached to this supplement, and provided to the Prosecutor's Office and the sentencing judge for their review.

STATUS: CLOSED, turned over to the Prosecuting Attorney

SUBMITTED BY: DETECTIVE TROMBLEY, GTSO/992 (03/31/03)

MT/tlm (03/31/03 @ 10:53 hours)

GRAND TRAVERSE LAW ENFORCEMENT SERVICES

STATEMENT

DATE: 03-26-08 TIME: 8:00 pm [signature] (SIGNATURE)

LOCATION: G.T.C.S.O

MY NAME IS: Shawn Priest

I AM 22 YEARS OF AGE. MY DATE OF BIRTH IS: 1-11-86

I LIVE AT: 1208 Allen Rd T.C. 49686 PHONE # (231)-941-1810

1993 - South Lake Tahoe Nevada -
In 1993 Chriss Timm Had Come Home from
a night of drinking with Local friends and
Stated that he needed to talk about Something
that happend a Couple of years previous. I was
unsure of what he was going to Say but
he looked very nervous and on edge. The
Conversation was about a accident that he
was in, involving Three deaths. I knew of what
he was talking about because I was at the
party the night before. His eyes Started to well
up and at that point He Said that he thinks
that he might of been driving the night that
the accident happend. He became very Shifty

[signature]

Page ______ of ______ (Signature) Rev.1/98

LE0013

after I asked him why He didnt Say anything to the Police about this. I don't really remember What his exact words were but Something along the line of his family being upset because one of the victims was his Cousin. The Conversation Basically ended when a Couple of people Stopped by to Say Hello. After that night it was never brought up again.

I really wouldn't be Suprised if he denied or Couldn't remember that Conversation we had about that insident.

Page ____ of ____ Signature: [illegible]

LE0356(a)

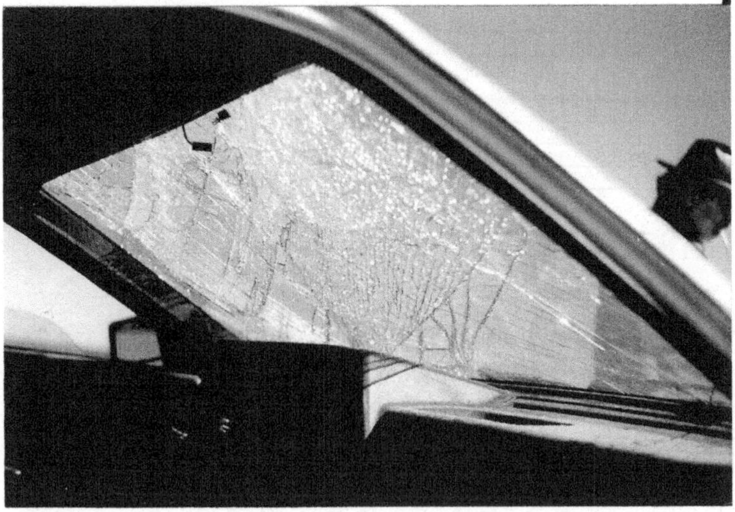

My son the poster boy. This picture was almost the cover of my book.

TRAVERSE CITY RECORD-EAGLE SECTION B

REGION

NEWS FROM NORTHWEST LOWER MICHIGAN

Sunday, September 14, 2003 NEWS TIP LINE (231) 933-1472

FATAL 1993 CRASH

Parole denied for driver

Jash Lardie's request for new trial denied

BY PATRICK SULLIVAN
Record-Eagle staff writer

TRAVERSE CITY — Jash Eli Lardie will remain in prison rather than admit he was the driver who caused a drunken crash 10 years ago that killed three teenagers.

Lardie, 28, was denied parole this month after he faced a parole board for a second time in two years — and for a second time maintained he was not responsible for the May 23, 1993, crash.

Lardie will be eligible for release again in early 2005.

Lardie was 17 at the time of the crash and is serving a six- to 15-year sentence after a jury convicted him in 1996 of three counts of drunken driving causing death.

Killed were Jason Stutesman, 17, Kendra Tiernan, 15, and Erinn Tompkins, 17.

Earlier this year Circuit Judge Philip Rodgers ruled against a motion Lardie filed for a new trial based on new evidence he said proved he was not the driver.

Lardie's refusal to admit responsibility, which relatives of the victims have said in the past has caused them great anguish, is not the first time he has rankled the court system and the community.

Rodgers originally sentenced Lardie to a year in the county jail and five years probation, but Lardie was not able to abide by some of the conditions.

Jash Lardie in 1993, left, and today.

He refused to sign a probation order. He defied a judge's order to stop sending letters about his newfound religious beliefs to families of the victims. And he outraged the community by refusing to accept responsibility for his crime.

Rodgers, who drew heavy criticism when he initially sentenced Lardie to a year in jail, then ordered him to serve six to 15 years in prison at a probation violation hearing in 1997.

Although no one from the parole board will discus its decisions, it's likely Lardie was denied because he has not admitted he caused the single-car crash, people familiar with the case say.

Gail Madziar, spokesperson for the Michigan Department of Corrections, said an inmate's refusal to admit guilt is grounds for denial of parole.

Rodgers agreed to comment about the case because he no longer presides over it. He said he wrote to the parole board before Lardie's first appearance two years ago about his concern over Lardie's lack of remorse, but he said he did not get involved in the board's recent decision.

"Unfortunately, what Mr. Lardie has demonstrated to me over the years is an almost pathological belief that he is innocent, that people would realize he's innocent and that, like Jesus, he would forgive them," Rodgers said.

Rodgers said that several years ago Lardie sent him a drawing of a hand, presumably Lardie's, nailed to a section of a cross.

Lardie insists he is innocent, even though he told police at the time of the crash that he had no memory of what happened.

Lardie's father, Jeff Lardie, said he has talked to his son about the possibility that if he took responsibility and showed remorse he could be released from prison. Lardie is not going to do that, he said.

"That would be lying to him," Jeff Lardie said.

Lardie's new trial motion this year included a claim

PLEASE SEE PAGE 2B

REGION/STATE

CRASH

Parole denied for man convicted in '93 fatal crash

FROM PAGE 1B

that he discovered evidence to prove he didn't drive the 1987 Nissan that rolled over and crashed into a tree on Peninsula Drive.

Lardie and the other teens had been at a party at Lardie's parents' house on Seven Hills Road. According to testimony at Lardie's trial, the party quickly grew out of hand as dozens of teenagers arrived to drink beer and whiskey at a bonfire behind the house.

In his motion, and at his trial, Lardie says he believes the actual driver of the car was the crash's only other survivor, Christopher Timm.

Police who investigated the accident disputed that theory. They noted that hair that appeared to belong to Lardie was found in the windshield in front of the driver's seat. Hair that apparently belonged to Timm was found in the windshield in front of the passenger

"Unfortunately, what Mr. Lardie has demonstrated to me over the years is an almost pathological belief that he is innocent. ..."

Judge Philip Rodgers

sear, police said.

This summer, detectives from the Grand Traverse Sheriff's Department investigated a claim that Lardie's brother had a chance encounter with a witness in the case, an acquaintance of Timm.

According to a police report, the witness said Timm admitted to him in late 1993 during a late-night, drunken conversation that Timm believed he was the driver of the car. Detectives — and the Record-Eagle — could not locate Timm.

Rodgers refused Lardie's motion, saying the new evidence was not trustworthy.

Families of the victims could not be located for this article, but some of them have spoken publicly in the past about the anguish they have suffered because Lardie has not shown remorse.

American Bar Association Criminal Justice Section Standards

Prosecution Function

Standard 3- 1.2 The Function of the Prosecutor

a) The office of prosecutor is charged with responsibility for prosecutions in its jurisdiction.

b) The prosecutor is an administrator of justice, an advocate, and an officer of the court; the prosecutor must exercise sound discretion in the performance of his or her functions.

c) The duty of the prosecutor is to seek justice, not merely to convict.

d) It is an important function of the prosecutor to seek to reform and improve the administration of criminal justice. When inadequacies or injustices in the substantive or procedural law come to the prosecutor's attention, he or she should stimulate efforts for remedial action.

e) It is the duty of the prosecutor to know and be guided by the standards of professional conduct as defined by applicable professional traditions, ethical codes, and law in the prosecutor's jurisdiction. The prosecutor should make use of the guidance afforded by an advisory council of the kind described in standard 4-1.5.

The prosecutor's duty is to seek justice, not merely to convict. This sounds good on paper, but I have not seen the prosecutor in my case very concerned about justice. He was just out for a conviction.

Passion Week
The Last Supper
Palm Sunday
The Garden of Gethsemane
The Betrayl and Arrest
The Trial
The Cross
The Crucifixion
The Death and Burial
The Resurrection

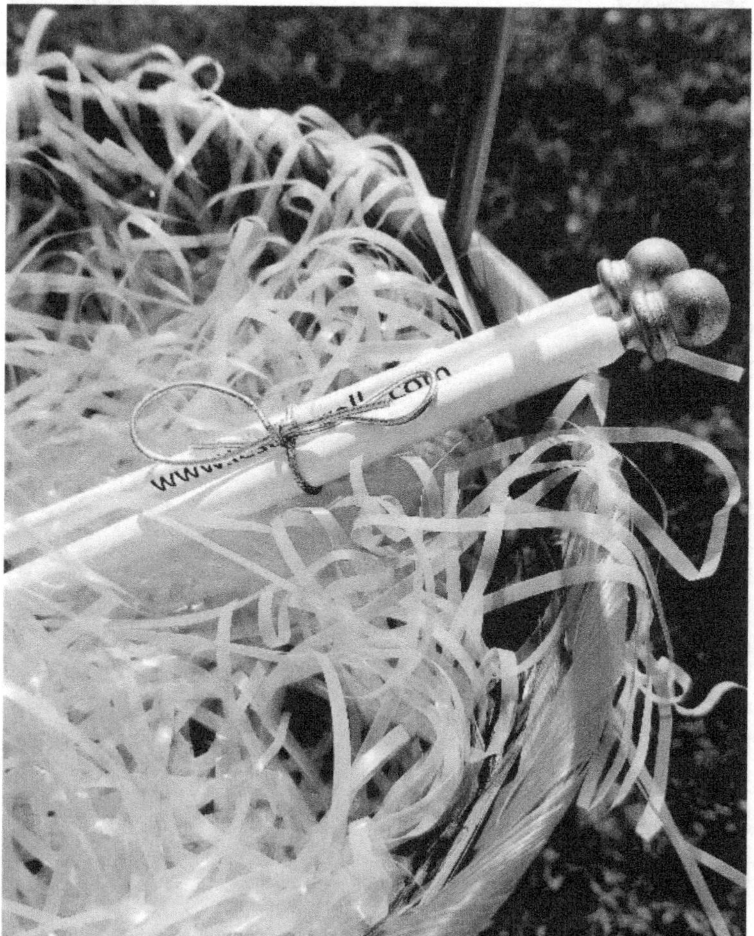

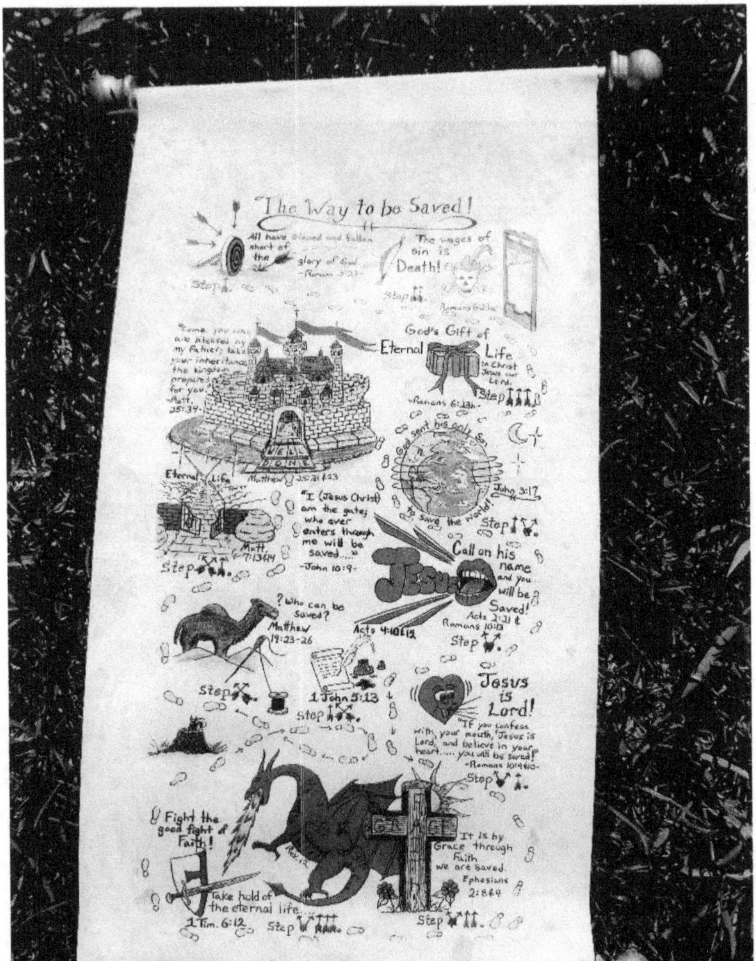

The Easter Scroll I made. The front side shows Jesus' last week on earth. The back side shows the way to be saved!

Made in the USA
Monee, IL
25 June 2025

19865087R00197